MASTERS SWIMMING – A MANUAL

DEDICATIONS

To Eric and Bonnie,
forever my beautiful kids.
Thank you for swimming with me.
From Blythe

To my wonderful children Nils and Hanna-Tineke
who always put up with my swimming.
From Cornelia

To all the swimmers and coaches who have touched our lives.
From Both of Us

MASTERS
SWIMMING

A MANUAL

LUCERO/BLEUL-GOHLKE

MEYER
& MEYER
SPORT

British Library Cataloguing in Publication Data
A catalogue record for this book is available from the British Library

Blythe Lucero/Cornelia Bleul-Gohlke
MASTERS SWIMMING – A MANUAL
Oxford: Meyer & Meyer Sport (UK) Ltd., 2006
ISBN-10: 1-84126-185-8
ISBN-13: 978-1-84126-185-0

© 2006 by Meyer & Meyer Sport (UK) Ltd.
Aachen, Adelaide, Auckland, Budapest, Graz, Johannesburg, New York,
Olten (CH), Oxford, Singapore, Toronto
Member of the World
Sports Publishers' Association (WSPA)
www.w-s-p-a.org

Printed and bound by: B.O.S.S Druck und Medien GmbH, Germany
ISBN-10: 1-84126-185-8
ISBN-13: 978-1-84126-185-0
E-Mail: verlag@m-m-sports.com
www.m-m-sports.com

TABLE OF CONTENTS

Table of Contents

FOREWORD

When I was growing up in competitive swimming in the late 1960s and early 70s, my heroes included the fastest swimmers of the time, not so much for their strength and power, but more for their tremendous dedication to perfecting their skill. Those swimmers knew how to move through the water! I studied their swimming and came to the conclusion that what made them great was their ability to understand of how swimming works, to focus on what needed to be done, and to put it all together in competition. Like me, those swimmers loved to swim, and they loved to swim well. Now, three decades later, as a swim coach, I still look at these qualities with awe when I observe them in a swimmer. They were immediately apparent in Conny.

When she found our swim team, she was struggling to adjust to life in the United States. Although she was comfortable with the English language, it was clear she was uncomfortable with her new surroundings. She looked worried and thin when I met her. In our initial conversation, I learned that swimming had been a big part of her life in Germany. As she looked longingly at the pool, I felt that she was truly a fish out of water. When I invited her to get in, her eyes twinkled, and she dove in without hardly interrupting the water. I knew then that, whether in Berlin or Berkeley, the water was her home.

Her swimming was relaxed yet powerful. She had versatility, polish, and she had speed! Above all, it was clear that she loved to swim and to do it well. She took great pleasure in the process of doing the workout. She did each set with purpose. As she swam, I saw clearly the qualities I admired in the great swimmers of my youth. Conny swam with heart. As I watched her, the hair on my arms stood on end!

It wasn't until later that I learned that she was both European and World Champion in several events. She was, and still is, truly one of the best female Masters swimmers in the world. Now after several years with our team, I can only say what a pleasure it has been to be involved in the swimming of such an athlete. She brings an enviable commitment to the sport, and a real appreciation for our program.

As a swimmer and as a person, she has become a part of the family of our team.

Of the many highlights of my coaching career, one of the most memorable experiences happened at the Short Course Nationals of 2003, under the blazing sun of Arizona. It was a great meet for our whole team, with many best times and medals. Conny was in peak physical condition and, looking like an athlete half her age, started out the meet by winning the 400 I.M., coming from behind in Lane 8 to the cheers of her teammates and me. She followed up that performance with a victory in the 200 breaststroke, leading the field solidly after the first 100, and never letting go. Shortly before her final event, the 200 I.M., as I was wilting in the relentless temperature of the final day of the meet, Conny turned to me and said, "You know, the heat is another competitor." This statement said it all to me. I knew then that she was going to swim the race of her lifetime. Sure enough, she approached the block with an intensity I had never seen. In the fastest heat, I watched her take on the eight length race with focus, understanding, and heart. I watched her reach inside and put it all together in an unforgettable swimming performance that was not only her best, but the best. After the meet, as I was still glowing from the successes of the swimmers on our team, Conny amazed me once more. She said thank you to me for her swimming.

It is with the utmost respect that I have worked on this book project with Conny. Our relationship over the past several years has enriched me as a person and inspired me as a swimming coach. It is my hope that swimmers and coaches who read this book will find their experience with Masters swimming to be equally meaningful.

Coach Blythe Lucero

When I met Coach Blythe for the first time at workout she was late. Another swimmer took me by the hand saying that she would come soon and just to warm up a bit. That was at an outdoor pool in Berkeley, California in November 2002. I had just moved to the United States. I was already an experienced and successful Masters swimmer in Germany. In fact, I had been on a swim team since I was a child, but never one dedicated only to Masters, with its own coach.

Some swimmers were warming up and some others introduced themselves to me. They ranged in age from 20 to 65, I guessed, and were all very kind. Then she came. An ageless-looking women with immensely long blond hair stepped confidently through the door to the pool deck greeting everybody by asking them if they'd already warmed up. "We have a new good swimmer here for our team," the girl who had guided me through the locker rooms announced, although I was still dry, standing on the deck. Blythe introduced herself to me and we talked a bit about my former swimming career, but she could see how eager I was to get in the pool.

It was one of the nicest and most pleasurable workouts I had ever swum and, after more than 32 years of swimming, you can guess how many workouts I have done. Not only was it that the pool was unexpectedly warm and the California air so refreshing, it was that every minute, every yard, every set of the training was a pleasure. And it has been like this for me ever since.

But why? Why is swimming with this Masters team so different?

Because of her! It didn't take long to find out why Blythe makes your day into a good one with every workout she provides. She just has the right feeling for everything concerning swimming. And I don't just mean her diversified workout plans, or that she is always on deck with the swimmers. No, it is the warmness, the humanness, the love with which she approaches so many different characters on the team, with so many different histories (in swimming and in private life) and such different expectations regarding swimming. She has all this and, together with her immense knowledge and experience of swimming, she gives it so generously and unselfishly to everybody who comes to swim. She doesn't want anything back and is just content seeing everybody swimming their laps fast or slow, improving technique and conditioning and leaving the pool pleasantly fatigued and satisfied. She has a word and an ear for everybody, no matter if it is about swimming or something else. She is the reason people find their way back to the pool and swim even if they are pregnant, have kids and family duties, were seriously ill, divorced or have been going though other problems. Afterwards, they feel better and are able to face their situations with more confidence.

This is the magic of Blythe's coaching, and that's why we have such a nice team whose members can swim together at the same time in the same pool despite being age 20 to 70 and older, coming from very different nationalities, or swimming on different levels. We may not be the largest team, or the one with the most record holders, but we have the best team.

It is a gift to have such a coach, even though I am not 16 anymore or on a college scholarship. I'm very grateful for this. It is also an honor for me to have worked on this book with Blythe. I hope and wish that everyone who reads this book will get the most benefit out of our work and partnership, not only in terms of swimming.

Keep swimming, Masters swimmers! Keep coaching, Masters coaches!

Cornelia Bleul-Gohlke

INTRODUCTION

Welcome to the world of Masters swimming. This book, written jointly by a Masters coach and a Masters swimmer, springs from the love of swimming. Throughout the development of this book, swimming has been a daily part of the process. It has invigorated us, challenged us, comforted us, and made us feel complete. As we continue to enjoy swimming, we are constantly amazed at the many ways that swimming improves our quality of life. We are older but we are healthy! The lifelong relationship each of us has enjoyed with this sport has been a strong influence in our development as people. As adults, it continues to impact the way we approach life.

This book is designed for swimmers and coaches: for those who are currently involved in Masters swimming, and for those considering entering Masters swimming, either as a first-time experience, or as reemerging athletes and coaches.

No Previous Competitive Swimming Experience Required
This book is designed to guide novice swimmers into life as Masters swimmers and to help make their swimming more efficient and enjoyable along the way.

Come Back to Life in the Fast Lane
This book is designed to inspire former competitors to return to their domain without many of the pressures they remember, but all of the excitement and opportunities for competition, if they want it.

How to Shake "Tin Man Syndrome"
This book is designed to encourage sedentary people of all ages to take up the lifestyle of Masters swimming to improve their flexibility, muscle tone and cardiovascular health.

Fun, Friends, Fitness
This book is designed to motivate fitness swimmers to new horizons, while enriching their social lives through friendships, special events and the team aspects of Masters swimming.

Masters Swim Team Seeks Coach

This book is designed to share with coaches the rewards and the challenges of forming and running a successful Masters swimming program, including issues unique to adult swimming.

Throughout the pages of this book, we have attempted to share our combined 60–some years of life in swimming with the reader in a way that celebrates, guides and inspires him or her to the full spectrum of Masters swimming.

In Chapter 1, the phenomenon of Masters swimming is described as a viable and beneficial fitness activity for adults of all ages, while the social aspects are revealed as one of its main attractions. The reader will find a bit of himself or herself through a series of true stories about Masters swimmers. A history of the birth and development of Masters swimming completes this chapter.

Chapter 2 offers a basic introduction to swimmer's equipment and the swimming environment. The reader will also learn about lane etiquitte, swimming jargon, sun sense, understanding pain, and swimming with health limitations. Swimmers will approach Masters swimming ready to swim for life!

Chapter 3 covers the important relationship between technique and conditioning. Each of the four competitive swimming strokes is described in detail and illustrated in a series of diagrams. A troubleshooting section accompanies each stroke section. An overview of the process of conditioning and sections on the elements of a workout and dry land training are included to assist in the development of better swimming.

In Chapter 4, the focus is on the team aspects of Masters swimming. The reader will learn how to find a Masters swim team that fits his or her expectations. In addition, this chapter looks at how to start a new team and the many issues involved in operating it successfully. The unique aspects of coaching adult swimmers and swim teams are also addressed.

In the final chapter, subjects include motivation and establishing a swimming routine. The thought process of swimmers as they move from one level to the next is described. Measuring progress is discussed in terms of physical improvements, goal setting and challenges in both competition and workout. Sticking with it, through the initial stages of swimming, is identified as a swimmer's biggest challenge.

LINK Throughout this book, a system of *links* in the margin has been included to make it easy for the reader to cross-reference information found elsewhere in the text. As so many swimming issues are interrelated, we thought this was an important element to add.

It has been our goal to create a user-friendly book, which makes Masters swimming approachable to all adults interested in improving, regaining and maintaining fitness. We hope you enjoy our book, and we hope you use it to build a lasting relationship with Masters swimming.

Finally, we want to acknowledge the many supporters of this project, including our families who believed in us; Vince who read each chapter-in-progress late into the night; Meredith and Jessica who edited with great care and skill; Steve and Kurt for their expert photography; Tami for being such a team player, and all the talented swimmers of Berkeley Aquatic Masters whose images grace the pages of this book.

CHAPTER 1
TAKE THE PLUNGE!

1 Why Masters Swimming?

1.1 ADULT FITNESS

Over the past few decades, the worldwide movement toward adult fitness reflects the growing sentiment that staying fit is not something that has to end with childhood. Until recently, it was only the elite athlete who was afforded the social acceptance to continue an athletic lifestyle into his or her adult years. And still, with a few exceptions, professional ball players, cyclists, weightlifters, runners and swimmers retired long before they were "middle aged." But the recent rise of adult fitness programs and associations, such as Masters swimming, have created not only more opportunities for adults to be physically fit, but have helped change the way society looks at adult fitness. Until very recently, adults who continued to pursue fitness with more than a casual interest were seen as aging people refusing to let go of their youth, unable to accept "growing again gracefully." Slowly, but surely, this attitude is changing.

It is more common to hear of adults involved in physical fitness described with esteem rather than ridicule, and more and more credence is given to the saying "you are only as old as you feel." Physically fit adults in their 30s, 40s, 50s, 60s, 70s and beyond are now called "adult athletes" by the evolved bystander, as they continue to defy athletic barriers.

Still, participating in a fitness routine as an adult takes some personal initiative and persistence. Masters swimming has become one of the most widespread adult fitness activities, with an international network of places to swim and events, making it both accessible and popular. But, beyond the issues of logistics and social acceptance, there are several hurdles that must be overcome to make fitness as an adult a true lifestyle.

HURDLE #1
Other Priorities

In adulthood, career and family take center stage. Time constraints are the norm, and the stress of adding one more element to the mix, such as a personal fitness routine, can be daunting. Often it seems that in order to add in fitness, something else has to be sacrificed.

In reality, this sacrifice is already taking place: your fitness is being sacrificed so that all the other priorities can be met. Now, no one is suggesting shirking work and family responsibilities in order to take up a fitness routine. This point is made very well by the pre-takeoff safety talk heard when travelling by airplane. In describing the proper use of the oxygen mask the flight attendant instructs the traveler to secure his or her own mask, before helping children and others. Why? Because if we do not take care of ourselves, we are useless to others.

Taking care of ourselves is truly the best way to ensure that we will be there to take care of the people and responsibilities in our lives. In addition to cardiovascular health, weight control and muscle tone, study upon study has shown a decrease in stress and an increase in energy and productivity directly attributable to physical fitness. Swimming in particular is cited by many of these studies as the single most beneficial fitness activity for adults, due to its longevity as a viable activity, as well as the low incidence of negative affects associated with it.

The bottom line is time management. Finding an hour or so in the day, three to four days a week is a challenge. Some people find it before work, some at lunchtime, others find that hour on the way home from work. Some people do it with their children nearby, some do it in rotation with their spouse, some even do it with their cell phone or pager on the edge of the pool. All in all, making the time to devote to one's own fitness is a decisive way to improve quality of life over the long term.

HURDLE #2
Breaking out of the Sedentary Lifestyle

It is an accepted fact that human beings reach their physical peak around the age of 18 to 21, and that after that age, the natural aging process leads to a slow decline in strength, endurance, speed and flexibility. But is the rate of this natural aging process related more to chronological age or physiological age? We all know 55-year-olds who can jump higher, run faster, and swim farther than some 30-year-olds. The crucial factor in the natural aging process is activity level.

By the time we reach our 20s, without maintaining the physical activity level of our youth, the growth of fast twitch muscle fiber decreases, weight gain occurs as metabolism slows, cardiovascular ability declines, and joints stiffen.

Now those people who have maintained an active lifestyle without a break since they were teenagers will have little adjustment to make when taking up an activity like Masters swimming. But for most of us, this is not the case. For most of us, a sedentary lifestyle has taken hold. From working at a desk all day, to child bearing and rearing, our level of physical activity is far less than it was when we were younger. Regaining a physically active body is surely a challenge but not an insurmountable one.

Breaking free of a sedentary lifestyle is not something that will yield immediate results. It is a process of rebuilding, and it will take time. The longer the break, the longer it can take. But remember, in taking on the lifestyle of an adult athlete, it is not only the goal that is important, it is the process. The hardest part is to take the first step...or stroke. Swimming is an ideal fitness activity for adults who have been sedentary for any length of time. The non-impact nature of swimming makes joint pain less of an issue during activity. The reduced gravity environment of the water means that weight gain is not as much of a hindrance as it is in many other sports. Because swimming uses every major muscle group, cardiovascular benefits begin right away. Stroke by stroke you can swim your way to fitness.

HURDLE #3
Making a Commitment

Becoming motivated to take up a fitness routine as an adult, such as Masters swimming is one half in making a commitment. Staying motivated is the other. Making a commitment means you are in for the long haul. And it won't always be easy. Things will get in your way. There will be disruptions to your routine. Measurable results may be hard for you to see sometimes. You might become tired, discouraged, and maybe sore at first.

Taking one day at a time is essential. Be forgiving to yourself. If you miss a day, oh well! One day will not make or break your fitness routine. Getting back on track is an important part of maintaining your commitment.

Remember, there is no timetable. Avoid making goals that measure success and failure, like: "By March 15, I am going to swim 100 yards in a minute." Choose instead to measure your progress with statements such as: "At first it took me 22 strokes to cross the pool, now it only takes me 18."

Let things develop, and believe in what you are doing. Never give up. Enjoy the process of building your fitness. Take pride in yourself.

Are you ready to make a commitment? Come on, take the plunge!

1.2 MASTERS SWIMMING VS. LAP SWIM

So you have decided to take up swimming as your adult fitness routine. You have taken the steps of making time in your schedule, and have found a convenient swimming pool. Now what?

Most pools offer Lap Swim, when the pool is open for swimmers to basically do their own thing. Many lap swims are organized into sections for slower, medium and faster swimmers. Lap swims usually have a lane pattern so that swimmers, like drivers on the road, do not bump into each other while they share a lane. Lap swimming offers swimmers the opportunity to swim at their own pace, swim what and how they choose to, and stop and go when they want.

There are drawbacks however. Lap swims can get crowded, and with everyone's perception of "fast" and "slow" being different, lane congestion can develop, leading to impatience by some swimmers, comparable to "road rage." Each lap swimmer's routine is different. For instance, while you might want to swim 20 lengths without stopping, the person in front of you might want to stop at the wall after each length for a minute or two. You may be swimming the breaststroke, and the person behind you is tailgating you doing freestyle. Lap swim can be frustrating for many swimmers. Others find the lap swim environment perfectly acceptable. It remains a popular program at many pools.

Deciding what to swim is the next issue. You could just get in and swim back and forth for the entire time you have set aside for your swimming. You could create your own routine of various strokes and distances. But what sort of swimming activities will help develop fitness best and most quickly? Choosing the best swimming activities is a difficult task for many swimmers and can easily lead to time wasted, lack of focus, boredom and loss of motivation. Even for the experienced swimmer, creating a workout and then doing it is a challenge and a hard routine to stick to.

The alternative is the Masters swimming environment that offers many benefits that lap swim does not. In Masters swimming, a structured workout is provided, other swimmers do that workout with you, and feedback is available about your swimming. For many swimmers, joining a Masters swim team has been an important factor in staying with their swimming routine.

Having the workout provided by a coach changes the activity from just swimming into training. The challenge of doing the workout from start to finish is quite appealing to many swimmers. Experienced Masters swim coaches create workouts designed to build endurance, speed and versatility, and improve technique. Workouts are planned with enough variety to keep swimmers engaged during the workout and interested enough to come back for subsequent workouts. Some Masters swim teams have themed workouts for each day of the week, for instance "Fin Monday" or "Sprint Friday." Some teams offer special workouts for seniors, commuters and other groups.

Doing the workout with other swimmers is very motivating to most people. With the workout as a common activity, swimmers usually find that they swim with more energy than they would by themselves. Being with a group of swimmers who are all doing the same workout creates a supportive environment, as well as an opportunity for competition, for those who want it. In Masters swimming workouts, swimmers are usually grouped by speed, which leads to smoother running lanes.

Finally, the Masters swimming environment offers the opportunity for stroke improvement. Having a coach analyze your swimming and suggest ways to improve is extremely helpful. Then, thinking about the feedback you get also gives you something to concentrate on when you might instead be thinking about how hard the workout is. No matter what level swimmer you are, there are many ways you can improve your stroke. Swimming technique is studied and practiced by Olympic champions as much as it is by beginners. Improving your swimming technique will only make swimming easier and more enjoyable.

Masters swimming offers a program that swimmers can build upon through the structure and variety of coached workouts. Masters swimming offers a program swimmers can stick with through its team environment and common goals. And Masters swimming offers a program swimmers can grow with through feedback and stroke correction, which is an essential piece of better, more enjoyable swimming.

SOCIAL ASPECTS OF MASTERS SWIMMING $\quad$ 1.3

The strong social atmosphere present in many Masters swimming programs is a valued part of most swimmers' experience. Being part of a stable social group is something that often seems to get set aside in the busy lives of many adults. The camaraderie of Masters swimming begins during workout, and often blossoms into lasting friendships carried on beyond the pool. Masters swimmers socialize in many ways including:

Workout Style Conversation

An interesting phenomenon common to most Masters swimming workouts is a developing a conversation that is strung together by the sets of the workout. Each set is punctuated by another minute or

two in a continuing light-hearted dialogue, and then is suspended until the next rest break, where it is resumed seamlessly until the next set begins. Some interesting subjects covered by this kind of intellectual workout chat have included:

- How peanuts grow, and whether they are really nuts
- The best places to travel in the Caribbean
- Menopause
- The role siblings order plays in personality traits
- Do watermelons float
- Good dentists
- Features of new water heaters

Social Kicking

Whether or not you believe that kick boards are beneficial to swimming, they play an important role in Masters swimming. During social kicking sets, swimmers kick side by side, catching up on news and making weekend plans. Conversations are also carried out across the pool, one swimmer kicking in Lane 2 and the other in Lane 6. Jokes are shared. Dinner dates are made. "Happy birthday" is sung. All this goes on while swimmers are in motion, propelled by

their leg action and floppy feet, accomplishing 200 or more yards of kicking, building their fitness while they build their friendships.

Aquatic Networking

At one point, there might be three architects, four teachers, two doctors, and three attorneys swimming in the pool at once. This presents quite an opportunity for shop talk. There are also times when the skills of swimmers in transition, between jobs, are brought to the attention of other swimmer/professionals and swimmers who own small businesses.

The resources of the Masters swimmers in the pool at any one time are quite extensive. One swimmer's house might be painted by a house painter on the team. The car of one swimmer might have a stereo installed by an audio professional from the pool. A swimmer might even find a pet sitter at workout.

Food Talk

About three-quarters of the way through a workout, when calories are running low, the topic of conversation inevitably turns to food. Spontaneously, swimmers begin to describe their desired post-workout snack or special treat with immense enthusiasm. Among the delicacies that have been shared aloud, in order of frequency mentioned are:

- Pancakes
- Bananas
- Oatmeal
- Cheesecake
- Ice Cream

In a sport where athletes can burn upwards of 600 calories per hour, shared cravings during workout often result in a group outing to a café or restaurant afterward, or the exchange of recipes.

Making Friends

While Masters swimmers are each unique in personality, background, lifestyle and occupation, they are all joined by their swimming. This common ground becomes the base of many friendships. Shared experiences in the pool create a strong bond between swimmers. People who might never cross paths otherwise build strong relationships in the pool. Pool time creates a kind of springboard for  many lasting friendships outside the water. For many, the friendships made through swimming are a major reason to keep swimming.

Being Part of a Team

Masters swimming offers a sense of team that many adults have not experienced since they were children. Belonging to a team gives us a feeling of being part of something larger than ourselves. This group identity puts things into a different perspective for us. It gives us a further reason to strive for higher goals. "Doing it for the team" is a great feeling. It makes us press on, when alone we might quit. It makes us encourage each other. It makes us cheer!

2 A Brief History of Masters Swimming

Masters Swimming was so named following the lead of Masters Track & Field, one of the only associations representing adult athletes at the time. Many people are still confused by the name "Masters swimming," which brings to mind elite level athletics, rather than the more encompassing population that the association truly stands for. Some Masters swimmers have suggested that the name be changed to "Veteran Swimming" or "Adult Swimming" to be more accurate. But the way Masters began explains the name.

Masters swimming began when Captain Ransom J. Arthur had an idea to hold a swim meet for adults in Texas. Arthur, a Navy doctor, wanted to spark interest in swimming as fitness and encourage adults to take up the sport to maintain and improve their health. His idea was to bring together ex-competitive swimmers and Olympians of years past from all over the United States for the event in order to gain publicity for his cause. The swim meet drew overwhelming response from retired swimmers all over the world. And the event netted the media attention Captain Arthur was seeking.

His swim meet marked the official beginning of Masters swimming in the United States in May 1970, with the first Masters National Swimming Championships.

The Federation Internationale Natation, FINA, the international governing body of competitive swimming, followed suit, adding references to Masters swimming in its Rule Book as of 1972.

Today, Masters swimming is organized and active on five continents, in countries including: Argentina, Australia, Brazil, Canada, China, Denmark, Egypt, France, Germany, Great Britain, Hungary, Italy, Japan, Korea, Mexico, New Zealand, Peru, Scotland, Slovenia, South Africa, Spain, Sweden, Switzerland, the United Arab Emirates, and the United States.

In the United States alone, over 43,000 people registered with United States Masters Swimming in 2005. The same year, more than 450 swim teams and clubs also registered throughout the country. Masters swimming events are held all over the globe including a World Swimming Championship, held every other year, by a different country every time.

Masters swimming is a large organization, but it is based in grassroots activities. In the United States, the structure begins with individual teams of swimmers operating in towns and cities across the country. Each team operates under the umbrella of a regional swimming committee, which represents a geographical zone including Oceana, the Breadbasket, Dixie, Great Lakes, Northwest, Southwest, and Southcentral. Each zone functions under the guidelines of United States Masters swimming, the governing body of Masters Swimming in the United States.

The mission of United States Masters Swimming is simple. It is to promote fitness and health in adults by offering and supporting Masters swimming programs. The organization is dedicated to the premise that the lives of participants will be enhanced through aquatic physical conditioning and competitions among its members and those of other nations, in the spirit of good sportsmanship.

3 The Many Faces of Masters Swimming

Every Masters swimmer has a unique story. During many years of coaching, I have been privileged to share many of them.
Here are a few of the many faces of Masters swimming.

3.1 THE RETIRED CHAMPION

Larry, a busy attorney, is nearing 50. He drops in at workouts frequently, but not on any particular schedule, without commitment, and knocks out a couple thousand to ease his aching back. No sports bottle containing an electrolyte-balancing drink for him: coffee is his poolside beverage of choice. His swimming is flawless and graceful. He understands swimming like the back of his hand. "Nice backstroke, Larry!" I comment from the deck between sets. My words evoke a smile as he pushes off for some last sprints. Larry, you see, was a top college backstroker, about a quarter century ago. He swam in a relay with Mark Spitz. The years have not dimmed his talent, either. One day, I clocked him off the wall for a 100 backstroke. He swam the four lengths in under a minute, without breaking a sweat.

"So, Larry," I used to regularly ask him. "When am I going to see you in a meet?" His expression would change, from the carefree swimmer who is one with the water, to that of an over-worked professional, asked to do one more thing. "Not me," he would reply. "My swim meet days are over." Although his time as an elite collegiate athlete was punctuated by accolades and medals, his memories of the four-year experience left him with the mindset that he never, ever wants to swim like that again: the seemingly endless workouts, the thousands upon thousands of mindless yards day after day, the coach who was never satisfied, and the constant feeling of being tired yet being expected to perform with the best at competitions. Most of all, the total absence of joy is what Larry recalls, and he doesn't want to feel that way again.

Having been a swimmer in the same era of "no pain, no gain," and "the more yards, the better," I know this feeling well. But in my capacity as a Masters coach, one day I gently pressed the issue. "Larry, I'll make you a deal." His ears perked up, and I continued, "If you just keep swimming, I'll just keep coaching. And if we keep going until we are 60, we'll swim in a meet together, okay?" He got a kick out of the challenge, and laughed out loud. And then said, "You're on!"

So, we've made a pact. Larry will keep his aching back at bay, and I will keep his time in the water fun, then in ten years or so, we will create a new swim meet memory, a kinder, gentler one, which will perhaps leave the other one in the dust.

THE FITNESS SWIMMER

3.2

Diane swims religiously three days a week, arriving punctually at the beginning of the workout and leaving exactly an hour and a half later. She happily swims in Lane 2, where she has swum for six years, with familiar lane mates and a familiar low-key atmosphere. There is no judgment cast when someone in the lane does a one-arm butterfly or swims a set with fins. It is not looked at as "cheating" as it might be by some swimmers in other lanes. The swimmers in her lane are friendly and courteous, and cooperatively change their order, depending on the set, or the way each person is feeling that day.

Balancing her career and her family effectively, Diane is the mother of two kids who works 9 to 5 as a project manager. Swimming is what she calls "her own time," and she is content to swim on a comfortable interval, taking the second or third position in kicking sets, and being the caboose for pulling sets. Diane is happy to have a coach on deck but would be just as content doing a workout posted on a board, as long as her lane mates were doing it with her.

Although she has an ongoing interest in improving her stroke efficiency, Diane has no aspirations of moving up to Lane 3, breaking any records, or even participating in competition. As most Masters swimmers do, Diane swims for fitness. In fact, about 70% of Masters swimmers do not compete. Through her swimming, Diane is among only a small percentage of 40-something women to maintain a regular physical fitness routine. She does not add to the alarming statistics in the American epidemic of obesity. She is in impeccable physical condition and proudly shares that her teenage son has now taken up swimming.

To Diane, and members of Lane 2 everywhere, may swimming Masters continue to enrich your lives with fitness and friendships.

3·3 THE POST-COLLEGIATE ATHLETE

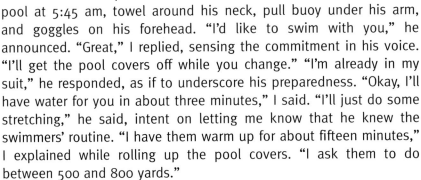

Jonas was waiting at the gate one morning when I arrived to open the pool at 5:45 am, towel around his neck, pull buoy under his arm, and goggles on his forehead. "I'd like to swim with you," he announced. "Great," I replied, sensing the commitment in his voice. "I'll get the pool covers off while you change." "I'm already in my suit," he responded, as if to underscore his preparedness. "Okay, I'll have water for you in about three minutes," I said. "I'll just do some stretching," he said, intent on letting me know that he knew the swimmers' routine. "I have them warm up for about fifteen minutes," I explained while rolling up the pool covers. "I ask them to do between 500 and 800 yards."

Soon enough, he was in the water, having chosen an outside lane even though it was clear that he had the speed. It was as if he was waiting for me to invite him to Lane 4, the lane reserved for the fastest swimmers. When he accomplished 1000 during warm up, I did ask him to join the fast lane. He started at the back of the line and worked his way, set by set up to the lead position. His swimming was powerful; the details were practiced. He put 100% into every set and didn't once miss his time on the pace clock. "So where did you swim?" I asked him between sets. He gave a quick resumé, which included four years at a Division 1 university and three years before that on the Swedish Nationals Team. He had just moved into town and been swimming consistently since college. He was clearly a freestyler/ backstroker, and he apologized that butterfly was not his strong point. He was no prima donna, communicating effectively but seriously about intervals and set details with the other swimmers in the lane.

At the end of workout, he was last to get out of the pool. When he hopped spryly out, he approached me. "So, can I swim with you?" he asked as if he had been trying out. Following his lead, I responded, "You made the cut!" He smiled and then proceeded to lay out the training schedule he intended to do. Curious, I asked him, "So what are your swimming goals?" "Just fitness," he replied decisively. "Okay," I said. "See you Wednesday morning."

So, Jonas made a routine of swimming with me, for fitness. After further inquiry, I learned that in college, he had been ranked among the top distance freestylers in the nation. Now, at age 30, I watched him take on 4 x 500 with descending 100 splits, and lactate threshold sets with purpose. But what purpose? Fitness? Both he and I knew this goal could be accomplished with much less effort. So, what was it? Unfinished business, I determined, after drawing out of him over time that he hadn't quite met his goals in college. This swimmer had something to prove to himself, and although it was yet to be defined aloud, he was building. And whatever shape the inevitable test takes, competition, or timed practice swim, Jonas has a mission, and it is a pleasure to be a part of it, and to believe in him every step of the way.

THE FIRST-TIME ATHLETE

3.4

Liz was a self-described nerd growing up. She was very focused on academics and got outstanding grades, leading her to receive a full scholarship to an Ivy League school. Again in college she excelled, earning double degrees in biology and international health. After graduation, she was the first pick of the largest biotech company on the west coast. Liz was well on her way.

By age 28, she had earned the esteem of her colleagues through her ground-breaking work in disease prevention. She was even quoted as an authority in her field in a *New York Times* about the strides in the biotech industry. With her career was established, Liz made a conscious decision to make a change in her life, to broaden her horizons, to do something completely new. She decided to take up Masters swimming.

With only the knowledge and experience of the mandatory high school swimming class she had taken ten years before, Liz researched Masters swimming in her vicinity, purchased a swim suit, goggles, and nose clip and showed up at a workout one Monday evening after work. She introduced herself and asked, "How good do you have to be to join this team?" I explained that our team was made up of swimmers of all levels and that previous competitive swimming experience was not required. She seemed to be relieved by my answer. I continued to give her an overview of the program. She told me that she really wanted to be a Masters swimmer and had already sent in her application to join the regional Masters swimming association.

When she got in the pool, she stood waist deep and spent a great deal of time adjusting her new goggles. Her nose clip was next, and then finally I watched her push off the bottom and swim head up freestyle for about half a length, then to the far wall doing breaststroke with scissor kick, still without getting her face wet. She rested on the wall for a while and then swam back toward me in the same way, snatching at the water with every stroke. She arrived exhausted. "So, may I make some comments about your stroke?" I asked her gently. "Yes, please!" she responded, eager to absorb any tips to help her gain the proficiency she was used to feeling in the rest of her life.

"Moving through water is a funny thing," I began. "It works best when we don't fight it." She was clearly curious. "The thing I think would help you most is to develop a good floating position." "Okay, how do I do that?" she urged me on. "It is important to hold your body in a streamlined position," I said, "including your head.

This means you have to swim with your face in the water, looking down at the bottom of the pool." "Okay, I can do that," she responded and submerged her whole head immediately. "Swimming with your face out of the water is like swimming uphill, and that is hard," I told her. I went on step by step to describe the basics of breathing while swimming, using long strokes, leverage, and effective kicking. She tried everything I offered.

"I had no idea that swimming was so technical," she said at the end of the workout. "Yes!" I replied, "There is a lot of science to good swimming." "Well, I should be good at that!" she stated confidently. "I'll be back tomorrow. Thank you!"

Liz swam in her first swim meet seven months after joining the team. She swam a 50 freestyle, including a flip turn. She swam it without her nose clip. She finished fifth out of six in her age group, and she was elated by her accomplishment as was I.

THE WEEKEND WARRIOR

3·5

Dale makes his appearance on Saturday and Sundays, swimming in Lane 3 on Saturday and usually Lane 2 on Sunday. He is a very outgoing guy and always greets his fellow swimmers cheerfully, as if he hasn't seen them in a week, which he hasn't. Dale's swimming speed is good enough to place him in the second fastest lane, largely because of his swim team experience in high school about twenty years ago.

Dale enjoys the workout setting of Masters swimming and the good-natured peer pressure of his lane mates during hard sets. Dale much prefers sprints to distance swimming. In sprint sets, he can maintain first or second position in his lane. During longer swims, however, he takes the rear. He knows that about halfway through a swim of 200 yards or more, he will need to stand up, and while pretending to adjust his goggles, allows his lane mates, who are catching up to him, to pass him up. On these longer swims, Dale stops when the group finishes, even though he still has two laps to go.

Near the end of workout, I watch Dale conscientiously tap the wall to start each 8 x 50, and then walk out ten yards before actually starting to swim.

Dale complains about shoulder problems when a set includes butterfly. It is only once in a while I've seen him do butterfly, and then for only a few strokes, before it turns into freestyle. I am sure that the shoulder pain he feels is real, not a way to avoid a strenuous set. But I also believe his pain is not from a technique problem, which is the first thing I analyze when a swimmer mentions shoulder problems. Instead, I am convinced it stems from infrequent, vigorous swimming, which is why by Sunday he joins the less intense folks in Lane 2.

"Dale," I say, "Can I get you to add a workout in the middle of the week?" "I only have weekends," he replies. I persist. "I really think a mid-week swim, even a short one, would help your shoulder stability." "I'm just too busy," he states. "Okay, then I'll give you some stretch band exercises to do during the week. They will really help you."

Dale thanks me with a smile, and continues to swim, as if I hadn't even brought it up.

3.6 THE OPEN WATER SWIMMER

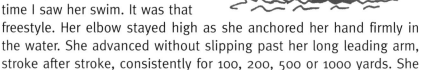

It wasn't Juliet's backstroke that impressed me the first time I saw her swim. It was that freestyle. Her elbow stayed high as she anchored her hand firmly in the water. She advanced without slipping past her long leading arm, stroke after stroke, consistently for 100, 200, 500 or 1000 yards. She seemed to gain speed as she swam, instead of settling into a pace, or running out of gas, which is physiologically more common.

Juliet had been lap swimming for exercise for a few months when she noticed my flyer on the bulletin board in the pool lobby that said in large print "Swimmers Wanted!" along with an invitation to adults of all ages to come join our Masters Swim Team. Juliet joined us with the idea that she would work toward equaling her high school 100 backstroke time, a challenge, but not an unattainable one. She was 25 years old, strong, lean and very determined. She enjoyed working out, she enjoyed swim meets, and she enjoyed challenges.

We worked on backstroke sets, and her time certainly did improve. She regularly placed in the top three in her age group at local competitions. But the meat and potatoes of each workout was freestyle. And hers got stronger and stronger. She was great at descending sets of 200s. Five, ten, or more, she swam them with precision, descending by a second or two each 200. Although sprint sets were not her forte, because she struggled to get her turnover up to speed quickly, she gave it her best just the same.

One day, a teammate brought a flyer to the workout announcing a rough-water swim across Lake Tahoe. It was a six-person relay swim, 11.5 miles across the lake, from Nevada to California. A boat was required to accompany each team, and in relay order the swimmers were to swim for half an hour each, then fifteen minutes each, and then ten minutes each, until they reached the finish line. Instantly, this is what everyone wanted to do, including Juliet. This was her debut into open water swimming.

Lake Tahoe was cold, about 55 degrees. It was windy and wavy, and hard to stay on course. While the high altitude slowed the swimming of about half the team, sea sickness took its toll on others. Then there was Juliet...she was in heaven! She felt a freedom she had never experienced in the pool. There were no walls to break her swimming rhythm, no laps to count, no constricting lane lines, just water as far as the eye could see.

Juliet was hooked! She entered every lake and ocean event announced, and by the end of her second season was ranked #2 in open water points in the region. As for the backstroke, she is still our medley relay lead-off swimmer, but her heart belongs to the open water.

3·7 THE TRIATHLETE

At age 50, Kurt has 3 percent body fat, and a resting heart rate of 40. He is an accomplished runner and cyclist, putting in hundreds of miles training each sport every month.

But swimming is another story. Seven years ago, when Kurt first appeared at a workout, he announced that he was going to do a Triathlon in four months, and that he wanted to improve his swimming for that reason. He told me that he had to be able to swim 2.4 miles by then, and that he would like my help. When he got in the water, I nearly jumped in after him when he approached the deep end. He was struggling.

Kurt was unarguably an athlete. He was strong, fit and able to do more than most 20 year olds … on land. But in the water, he flailed. Technique-wise, there was a lot I could help him with, but there were other issues that made swimming hard for him. Right away, I noticed that the flexibility of Kurt's feet only went in one direction, that of a runner and cyclist. The ligaments in the front of his ankle were so tight that he could not point his toes, making his kicking ineffective at best. I also noticed that Kurt's posture standing, and in the water, remained as if he was on a racing bike, hunched over at the shoulders. He had a hard time reaching his arm out straight, making streamlining a basic problem.

On the bright side, Kurt had excellent core strength, the muscle tone of a teenager, a thorough understanding of the principles of conditioning, and intense will power. I decided the best approach to help Kurt reach his goal was to work his strong points and work around his limitations. We worked on body roll and initiating his swimming from his hips so he could get the most from his strong core. We worked on body position so he wasn't exhausting himself kicking to keep his legs from sinking. We worked on aligning his arm stroke from his armpit to his thumb, in order to create a more effective catch phase in his stroke.

Kurt's drive and willingness to make changes led him to improve quickly. It wasn't long before he was swimming laps without stopping. We measured his efficiency by counting strokes per lap. He was able to develop what I call "quiet swimming," which was low on the excess splash. After three months, he was able to do a set of 20 x 50 and hold a steady pace. As the date of his triathlon event grew closer he asked me, "Do you think I can really do it?" "Yes, Kurt," I responded, "I do. I think you have made huge strides in your swimming in a very short time. You know what you have to do. You just have to swim like you have been practicing: long and efficient. It will be hard, but you have the endurance, and you have the skill." "Okay", he said with conviction.

Kurt came back two weeks later from Hawaii with a new Ironman tattoo around his ankle. "I did it!" he stated simply. "You did it, Kurt!" I echoed, my hand raised for a high five. After a minute of proud silence he said, "The next one is in six months. Are you up for it?" I was slightly taken aback by his question. It was as if I was the one in training. "You know, I really couldn't have done it without you, coach," he said in a quiet voice. I smiled and answered, "You just keep swimming, Mr. Ironman!" And he has. Kurt has competed in 14 triathlons in the past seven years. His swimming has improved consistently, with his 2.4-mile swim time now over 40 minutes faster than the first time he swam it in Hawaii.

THE RENAISANCE ATHLETE

3.8

It had been a while since Tami had taken on a swimming challenge with so much dedication.

The intensity of college swimming had been over for a few years. She had joined Masters swimming at age 23 just for fun and enjoyed the relaxed atmosphere and friendly company immensely. She attended workouts fairly regularly and had fun swimming without the pressures of college athletics.

Eventually though, it became clear that competition was still in her heart, and she set her sights on Masters Nationals. She dedicated herself to an intense training schedule, including weight lifting and "doubles," days where she did two workouts per day. She gave up sugar for ten weeks. She led her lane and worked her splits. She challenged herself in every way, inspiring other swimmers in the pool with her self-discipline.

When she emerged from the Master Swimming Short Course National Championships, she had a new bounce in her step, new confidence in her swimming, and the knowledge that all her work was worth it. Tami took off a total of more than 60 seconds in five events over the course of the meet!

She began with the 400 IM. She took the lead on the very first lap and never relinquished it. She turned in her best 100 fly and breaststroke times of the season as splits in the 400 IM! She finished the race in 5:11.96, eliminating 20 seconds from her entry time, placing 6th. Next, she swam the 50 fly. Matching her college time, she swam a 28.95, placing 10th.

Tami's father flew in from Los Angeles for the final two days of the meet, arriving just in time for Tami's 500 freestyle. Setting a fast pace early on, she finished the 20 pool lengths in 5:42.77, erasing another 20 seconds from her entry time and placing 9th. Then she swam the 100 fly, demolishing her time by six seconds, coming in at 1:02.70, 7th place, and very near to her best college time. Great!

The final day, she took her most challenging event head on: the 200 fly. With dreams, but no expectations, she took to the block. When the dust had cleared, Tami touched the wall in 3rd place in an amazing time of 2:17.78, a 14-second improvement that brought her back to her best year in college. A smile lit up her face. A competitor was reborn.

THE LIFELONG ATHLETE

3.9

Bernie has been voted "Most Inspirational Swimmer" unanimously by his teammates two years in a row. He is a very special person, who has befriended many of his teammates, frequently connecting with them outside the pool for plays, museum openings, conversations over gourmet coffee. He greets every swimmer by name, even if he has only met them once. He loves to celebrate holidays and brings a small trinket for the coach every Easter, Halloween and Christmas. Bernie has been described by his fellow swimmers as genuine, brotherly, and wise. He is a very important presence at our workouts. Bernie swims twice a day, without fail, putting in a good hour at each workout.

Before taking up swimming, he was a dedicated long distance runner, and had been since his youth. It was an essential part of his identity and athletic spirit, until his knees would no longer allow it. It was a sad day when he had to stop running.

I met Bernie one Saturday, when he dropped in on my Swimming Technique class, asking if I could give him some pointers on swimming the front crawl. He explained he had recently retired from running and that he wanted to try swimming as a way to stay active. Bernie was a muscular man, about 45, I guessed, with a humble manner about him.

He was comfortable with the water but not with his swimming. With his extensive endurance running background, there was no question that he could keep going with fifty or more strokes per length, but he was working too hard to enjoy swimming. As we developed his stroke, he contemplated every correction carefully, practiced, asked good questions, and practiced some more. He quickly became a regular at Masters workouts, in Lane 6, making friends, observing the other swimmers strokes, and sharing the techniques he had most recently incorporated into his stroke with his lane mates. Swimming became his new passion. Soon, with the encouragement of his teammates, he entered a local swim meet.

Bernie entered the 50 freestyle in the 65-69 age group! I was astonished. Not only was he the only swimmer on the block without silver hair and wrinkles, he was the only swimmer who sprinted! Bernie's years of running had preserved him well. There was no loss of muscle tone, no flexibility or posture indications that Bernie was a senior citizen. His body was young, except for his knees, and Masters swimming was just the sport for him to reap the rewards of being a lifelong athlete.

Bernie's performance at that first swim meet was the beginning of a bright new chapter in his life. He had found a new community, and he had found a way to let the athlete in him continue to live.

CHAPTER 2
MASTERS SWIMMING READINESS

1 Check in with Your Doctor

When you fill out the Masters Swimming Membership Application, you will be asked to acknowledge that you have been in contact with a physician and have been given the "okay" to participate in Masters swimming. Even without this requirement, letting your healthcare provider know that you plan to take up Masters swimming may seem unnecessary, but it is a wise idea. You will most likely make your doctor's day when you describe your intentions because you will be making a lifestyle change that will make you a healthier person. Your doctor knows that he or she will have to do less nagging about your weight, cholesterol, and blood pressure, among other issues when you swim regularly.

Any health concerns you or your doctor have can be discussed, including asthma, heart condition, diabetes, hypertension, osteoporosis, so you can make a plan to "swim around" these issues, rather than ignore them. By making such a plan, you will avoid the chance of becoming discouraged with the Masters swimming experience. Usually, even with health limitations, your doctor will be highly encouraging, as the benefits of swimming highly outweigh any risks. Expect your doctor to be pleased that you are taking positive steps to improve your health, then begin the experience of Masters swimming with confidence.

2 Equipment

2.1 SWIMSUIT

A distinction should be made between a bathing suit and a swimsuit. Whereas a bathing suit is selected largely for looks, as its purpose is for sun bathing, the swimsuit is designed for swimming. Function should be the primary consideration when selecting a swimsuit. Your swimsuit needs to fit snugly to avoid drag, but allow you to move comfortably and freely at full extension.

Swimsuits designed for training are now made of fabric that is resistant to chlorine, which is a great feature for frequent swimmers. Swimsuits designed for competition are made of high-tech fabric, which repels water and streamlines the body, as swimmers strive to shave off any possible drag. These competition suits are not designed to be worn everyday, as the fabric is not chlorine-resistant.

2.2 SWIM CAP

If you have long hair, a cap is a must in order to keep your hair out of your face while swimming. Hair can interfere with breathing, and it can restrict your arm movements if it is long enough to go under your arms while you stroke.

Even with short hair, many swimmers choose to wear a cap. A swim cap lessens drag. It keeps your head warm. It keeps the sun off your head. It also protects the hair somewhat from chlorine damage, although the hair does not stay dry under a cap.

2.3 GOGGLES

When many of us were kids, goggles were not an essential piece of our swim equipment. They had not been developed beyond the cumbersome scuba type masks, which covered the nose, making them inappropriate for competitive swimming. As youth swimmers, we went to school from swim practice with red, burning eyes, which lasted far into the day.

Now, goggles have been designed with competitive swimmers in mind, with features including adjustable nose bridge and head straps, UV protection, and a variety of shapes to fit just about anyone's face. You can even get prescription goggles for vision correction!

The goggles of today are light and comfortable. Swimmers do their whole workout with goggles, including backstroke. They compete with goggles, including diving. Red, burning eyes have become a thing of the past.

KICKBOARD

2.4

Some pools have kickboards for their patrons. If not, you may purchase your own kickboard, but check with the coach of the swim team that you are joining to see if kickboards are used. Some coaches believe that kickboards do not promote good body position in swimming, so they have their swimmers do kicking activities without kickboards.

Kickboards do provide floatation to the upper body and allow the swimmer to kick with their head out of the water, but some swimmers struggle to make forward progress when using them. If kickboards are a part of the team's program, choosing the appropriate kickboard is important. Select one that is no longer than the distance from your wrist to your armpit. Otherwise, the kickboard can be stressful to the shoulders, and an "uphill" kicking position is almost insured, making kicking more work.

A properly fitting kickboard makes kicking a pleasant variation from face in the water activities.

PULL BUOY

2.5

A pull buoy is a float held between the legs, above the knees. Some pools provide pull buoys for their patrons' use. The pull buoy is a favorite piece of equipment for many swimmers. It allows the upper body to be used, but floats the legs so no kicking is required. For some swimmers, a pull buoy corrects their floatation and body position to the point that pulling is actually easier than swimming.

Pull buoys come in a variety of styles and sizes. Swimmers can select the style they find most comfortable. The correct size of a pull buoy is determined by the swimmer's size and weight. A properly fitting pull buoy provides enough floatation so the swimmer's hips don't sink, but not so much that the lower back takes extra stress.

Some swimmers are able to pull well and comfortably without a pull buoy.

HAND PADDLES

2.6

Caution should be exercised when using hand paddles because, without proper stroke technique, the extra shoulder stress produced by using paddles can result in injury. Any shoulder pain should not be ignored! If even the slightest shoulder pain occurs, take the paddles off and ask for help with your stroke before using the paddles again. Paddles should be selected in the right size, which is only slightly larger than the hand. When they are too big, they can cause shoulder problems. Paddles are usually used while pulling and sometimes for swimming, too. Paddles are not often recommended for strokes other than freestyle. They should not be used for more than one quarter of a swimmer's workout.

Paddles are used to increase the resistance of the water, allowing the swimmer to work harder and to develop a more effective stroke path. While using paddles, the swimmer feels like he or she has more of a "handle" on the water. A swimmer can then try to replicate this "handle" when the paddles are taken off. Paddles are very beneficial for giving the swimmer immediate technique feedback on the entry and exit of the stroke. An incorrect motion in the water at these points will cause the paddle to pull off, showing the swimmer a specific problem area to work on.

2.7 FINS

Many coaches do not believe in fins because they feel that swimmers become dependent on them. Certainly, fins give a swimmer the feeling of speed, and going fast is fun. But going fast can also be a beneficial feeling for a swimmer to experience and then to strive for without fins. Fins should not be used for the majority of kicking activities or a swimmer may forget how to kick without them. Kicking with fins should always be faster than without fins because fins provide a larger surface area with which to move water. If you kick only the same speed as you go without fins, then you are not working as hard as you would without fins. This is not the point of wearing fins.

Fins can be used to help swimmers feel the importance of the kick in strokes where the kick is a frequent problem, including the butterfly and backstroke. Fins should not be used for breaststroke because the extra resistance produces too much stress on the knees.

If fins are a part of your swim team program, selecting the right fin is important. Even if fins are provided by the pool for patrons to use, it is a good idea to get your own. It is important for fins to fit absolutely correctly, or they will encourage incorrect kicking. The fin should not be too long. A long fin promotes a slower kick. Competitive swimmers need to kick fast, so choose a shorter fin. The fin should be fairly flexible, to simulate the fluid, tail-like effect that an ideal kick has. The fin should also not squeeze the foot, so that the swimmer holds back their effort, to avoid foot pain. Fins are fun, and they have benefits but remember that every swimmer should be comfortable kicking with his or her own feet!

2.8 WATER BOTTLE

Staying hydrated is the last thing many swimmers think about when they are surrounded by water. But even if you cannot feel yourself sweat, swimmers lose a great deal of water while they workout. For this reason, many swimmers bring water bottles with them to the edge of the pool. Many swimmers drink water. Some drink sports drinks containing minerals and sugar. Some swimmers drink solutions designed to help the body recover after workout.

3 Around the Pool

PACE CLOCK

3.1

The pace clock is a standard piece of equipment for any swim team workout. It is a large face clock, visible to swimmers in the pool. The pace clock has a second hand and a minute hand that swimmers use to get immediate feedback about the speed of their swimming. They can also time their rest. Before the pace clock was designed in the 1950s, by Doc Counsilman, a very influential American swim coach, swimmers depended on their coaches to call out their times, measure their rest, and to set them off on their next swim on schedule. In situations with more than a few swimmers in the pool at once, coaches were only able to get some of the swimmers' times accurately. Although many coaches still call out times, the pace clock allows swimmers to take charge of their workout.

The pace clock makes working out a more interactive activity. Swimmers are able to see all of their own swim times, stay on their interval, and check their pace. Many swimmers consider the pace clock to be their primary workout partner.

LANE LINES

3.2

Lane lines, or the floats strung together over the length of the pool, have three purposes. First, they divide the pool into areas, which allow more swimmers to swim in an organized and safe manner in a limited space. Second, they provide a guide for swimmers to swim more on course, especially in backstroke. Third, good lane lines can eliminate quite a bit of turbulence on the water's surface.

Lane lines are extremely expensive, and for this reason, swimmers are discouraged from hanging on them to rest or fix their goggles. They are not designed to hold a swimmer's weight, and if one breaks, the quality of everyone's workout suffers.

3.3 LINES ON THE BOTTOM OF THE POOL

Every pool designed for competition has black lines painted or set in tile on the pool floor. These lines work like lane dividers on the road and keep swimmers on course.

There is usually a "T" at both ends of each line, near the walls of the pool. This "T" is a signal to the swimmer that the wall is approaching and to prepare to finish or turn as the case may be.

On the wall of many pools, in alignment with the line on the bottom of the pool, is a "+" designed to give swimmers a target for turning. Some coaches discourage the use of this "+" because it encourages swimmers to look forward, instead of down, compromising their body position and slowing them down.

3.4 BACKSTROKE FLAGS

The colorful flags strung across the width of most pools about five yards out from the wall are not just there for decoration. They are backstroke flags, used to determine a swimmer's distance from the wall, and to prepare for the turn or finish.

Because the line on the bottom of the pool is not visible while the swimmer is on his or her back, backstroke flags are essential for swimming safely and swimming without slowing down to negotiate the wall.

Backstroke flags are hung at the standard distance from the wall of five yards at every competitive pool. By counting their strokes from the point they pass under the flags, swimmers develop the ability to finish and turn quickly without looking back at all. Backstroke flags allow swimmers to practice their turn and finish in one pool and have the same "count" in another pool.

POOL DEPTH MARKERS

3·5

Knowing how deep the water is that you are entering is a matter of safety. Most pools are not uniform in depth. Depth markers are usually printed on the edge of the pool or set in tile. Knowing the depth of the water advises swimmers in advance where they can stand up and where they can't. It also tells swimmers if diving is safe and appropriate, or if entering the water feet first is necessary.

Even experienced divers and swimmers who know how to do shallow racing dives are discouraged from diving into the shallow end of the pool. Diving accidents are the number one cause of permanent injury at swimming pools, and you do not want to risk becoming another statistic.

LIFEGUARDS

3·6

Many pools provide lifeguards during Masters workouts, as they do for other water activities. Some Masters coaches are also certified lifeguards. The primary job of lifeguards is to ensure safety, so preventing injuries before they happen is their main concern.

This sometimes requires a lifeguard to intervene in swimming activities. For instance, a lifeguard might help if a swimmer is about to dive into shallow water, when someone is swimming the wrong direction in the lane, or when a swimmer hangs on the lane lines.

The majority of lifeguards are younger than Masters swimmers. Lifeguarding is a job that carries the most responsibility that a young person can be hired to assume. Masters swimmers should remember that even though the lifeguard may be "a kid," it is important to respect the rules they enforce. They are there for your safety.

4 Lane Etiquette

Lane etiquette is highly developed in most Masters workouts. It allows more swimmers to swim together pleasantly and safely, in a well-organized, well-moving environment. For some swimmers, the lane etiquette of a Masters swimming workout is a major reason they have chosen Master swimming over lap swim.

Lane etiquette encompasses rules for swimming and guidelines for courteous behavior. Each team may have its own rules, so it is a good idea to get to know them. In general, the considerations include:

4.1 CHOOSING THE RIGHT LANE

Most Masters swimming workouts are organized into lanes where swimmers of similar speed are grouped together. This allows each lane to move smoothly with the least amount of slowing and passing. Having swimmers of the same speed do the workout together increases the quality and enjoyment of everyone's experience. Slower swimmers do not feel they are in the way, and faster swimmers do not feel they are pressuring other swimmers.

Choosing the right lane may be difficult at first, but after a while, a swimmer is able to gauge his or her speed and endurance and determine the best place to swim. If you are unsure of which group to swim in, ask the coach. If you choose a lane that turns out to be too fast or too slow, be ready to move to another lane. Remember, the goal is to keep each lane moving well, not to make anyone feel unwelcome.

4.2 WHO GOES FIRST?

Some swimmers are leaders. Some swimmers are followers. If you strive to lead your lane, you are striving to be the fastest, most consistent swimmer in that lane. Leading a lane carries a lot of responsibility with it. Lane leaders are expected to watch the clock carefully. They are expected to count laps accurately. They are expected to keep the lane moving at a speed that accommodates everyone. If you are new to an established lane, it is courteous to start at the back of the line and work your way forward, as your swimming skills speak for themselves. If you become the leader and finish consistently far in front of everyone, it might be time to move to a faster lane.

CIRCLE SWIMMING

4·3

Circle swimming is the most common pattern of organization in Masters swimming workouts. It allows the most people to swim in one lane without bumping into each other. It requires that all swimmers cooperate in swimming down on one side of the lane and back on the other side. It is important to know if the circle pattern starts on the left or the right before you begin swimming. Often, you can determine this by observing the swimmers. If you are unsure, asking your lane mates shows that you are aware of the circle swim practice and that you want to make your joining of their lane problem-free.

When circle swimming, details are important in keeping a smooth running lane. These details include:

Following Distance

Know how many seconds each swimmer is supposed to wait before starting to follow the swimmer in front of them. Commonly, swimmers leave the wall five seconds apart. In certain situations, ten seconds or more is set as the spacing. Ask what the custom is on your team, then use the pace clock to be accurate.

Turning

Turns can be especially problematic in lanes with several swimmers, because as swimmers swim close together, collisions are more likely while one person is pushing off the wall and another swimmer is approaching the wall.

Although the fastest turn is done straight in and straight out of the wall, in the circle swimming environment, this is not an option. Instead, swimmers approach the wall on their side of the lane, aim at the "+" on the wall just before they turn, and then push off diagonally in order to get over to the other side of the lane most quickly.

Passing

Even if all swimmers in a lane are about the same speed, passing becomes an issue especially during longer swims, as different levels of endurance become apparent. There are times when the lead swimmer may catch up to the last swimmer in the lane before the swim is finished. For these situations, rules of passing should be understood in advance by all swimmers in a lane.

Passing is not only the responsibility of faster swimmers. It must be done in cooperation with slower swimmers. Some teams call for passing only at the wall, when a slower swimmer stops for an instant while a faster swimmer swims by. Some teams call for a faster swimmer to signal a slower swimmer by tapping their feet, so the slower swimmer can move over and let the faster swimmer go by. Some teams call for a faster swimmer to change directions near the end of the lane, going in front of a slower swimmer without interruption. Knowing the passing customs of your team is important to keep the lane moving as smoothly as possible and to avoid any swimmer, slower or faster, becoming frustrated.

Collisions and Side Swipes

Sometimes, accidents happen. If you are involved in a collision or side swipe, acknowledge what happened and ask if the other swimmer is okay. This is courteous. There are situations when collisions are most common. These include any activity on the back, swimming, kicking or drilling. To avoid collisions when on the back, swimming close to the lane line is a good idea. "Hugging" the lane line will put the most space between you and another swimmer coming toward you.

There are also situations when side swipes are most common. These include when swimmers are doing butterfly, kicking breaststroke, using hand paddles, and when a swimmer has an especially wide freestyle recovery. Being aware of other swimmers' activities and whereabouts can prevent many problems. A simple one-armed stroke, or at least a purposeful narrow stroke, as you and another swimmer are passing by each other can reduce side swipe situations dramatically.

WHEN YOU ARRIVE LATE 4·4

Although sometimes unavoidable, when you arrive late to workout, it does cause an interruption to a lane already in progress. When you arrive late, do not expect to do a standard warm-up in a lane that has already completed its warm-up. You should simply join into the activity that they are doing and attempt to make that your warm-up. Do not interrupt the swimmers to get an explanation of what they are doing. If it is not clear what they are doing, wait until they stop for instructions, or ask the coach.

Be aware that the swimmers you are joining have already expended a great deal of energy at the workout, and it is only courteous to not take your swimming out very fast, as you are fresh, upsetting the rhythm of the lane. Some Masters swimming workouts have a designated warm-up lane, specifically for swimmers who arrive late. This is not the case for most teams though.

WHEN YOU HAVE TO LEAVE EARLY 4·5

Sometimes, leaving before the end of a workout is unavoidable. Be aware that your leaving does affect the way the lane works. When you leave in the middle of a set, swimmers behind you suddenly get less rest, as they are expected to move up in the order.

It is courteous to let your lane mates know in advance that you have to leave early. Try to leave after a set has ended to avoid interrupting your lane too much. Depart acknowledging with admiration that your lane mates are staying for the whole workout.

5 Workout Jargon

"Okay, twenty fifties on the forty five, every fourth one fly. On the top," the coach says. What the heck does that mean? Swimming jargon becomes easy to understand soon enough, but at first it almost sounds like a different language.

The translation of what the coach said is: Swimmers are to swim 50 yards, which is two lengths of the pool in a 25-yard pool, twenty times, leaving every 45 seconds on the pace clock, which includes swim and rest time, doing freestyle, except for the forth, eighth, twelfth, sixteenth and twentieth 50s, which are butterfly, and the first swimmer is to start when the second hand reaches sixty.

It is clear from the length of this translation why swimming jargon evolved. Common terms of swimming jargon include:

All out	As fast as you can
Breath Control	A breathing pattern that is less frequent than usual
Descending	Faster each time
Drill	An activity designed to emphasize one aspect of stroke technique.
50	Fifty yards/meters, or two lengths of a 25-yard pool, or one length of a 50-meter pool
50 Easy	A 50 yard/meter recovery swim
I.M.	Individual Medley. A continuous swim of butterfly, backstroke, breaststroke and freestyle in that order
I.M. order	Butterfly, backstroke, breaststroke and freestyle in that order
Interval	The combined swim and rest time that a swimmer holds in a set

Kick	Propulsion done by the legs
Lap	One roundtrip of two lengths of the pool. Also, commonly used synonomously with "length" in swimming
Length	The length of a pool from end to end
100	One hundred yards/meters, or four lengths of a 25-yard pool, or two lengths of a 50-meter pool
On the top	Leaving when the second hand reaches the :60 on the pace clock
On the bottom	Leaving when the second hand reaches the :30 on the pace clock
On the side	Leaving when the second hand reaches the :15 or :45 on the pace clock
Pull	Propulsion done by the arms and upper body
Race Pace	As fast as you would go in a race
Set	A series of repeated swims grouped together
Split	The time of a part of a swim. For instance, you could get ten 50-yard "splits" in a 500-yard swim
Streamline	The optimum body position to glide through the water with the least amount of drag
25	Twenty-five yards, or one length of a 25-yard pool
200	Two hundred yards/meters, or eight lengths of a 25-yard pool, or four lengths of a 50-meter pool

6 Under the Sun

The healthy glow of an outdoor swimmer is unmistakable and awed by many. But there are concerns for swimmers who regularly swim in the sun. The amount of time spent in the sun by many swimmers is both greater than recommended on a daily basis, and it is ongoing over the long term, as they continue to train outdoors. In addition, the sun's effects are intensified by the water at the same time as the swimmer is cooled by the water, giving a false impression of the amount of sun that the swimmer is getting. Without precautions, these issues present perfect conditions for sun damage. This damage can be as benign as wrinkled skin, and as serious as skin cancer or cataracts. Sun damage happens silently and gradually, sometimes with very serious results.

The key to dealing with extensive daily and long-term effects of sun exposure is prevention rather than damage control. Sunscreen is a must for swimmers who workout outside. There are waterproof varieties that will protect swimmers throughout their workout, reducing damage to the skin from premature aging and decreasing the real chance of developing skin cancer. The term skin cancer is deceptive. While the initial stage of melanoma, a very serious form of skin cancer, does emerge on the skin, giving a less serious connotation than its true deadly potential, it is important to know that the more advanced stages are invasive and can aggressively spread to tissue, organs and bone.

The eyes of outdoor swimmers are also especially vulnerable to damage. While historically appearing in later life, the incidence of cataracts is on the rise in younger adults at an alarming rate. They are occurring more and more frequently among outdoor swimmers, especially among those with light-colored eyes. Cataracts form as the lens in the eye gets cloudy, or dark, and vision is diminished, sometimes to the point of near blindness. This condition can be corrected surgically by removing the damaged lens and implanting a synthetic one. However, vision is not as good as it was before the cataracts developed. Avoiding exposure and risk of cataracts can be achieved by simply wearing dark tinted goggles with UV protection.

Coaches on the pool deck should also take precautions. Sunscreen, sunglasses and a brimmed hat should all be a part of their deck wear. The glare and reflective nature of the water can intensify the effects of the sun as much as if a person is in the water. Swimmers and coaches who spend regular periods of time in the sun can enjoy its positive effects, without suffering its negative consequences, when the proper care is taken in advance and practiced consistently.

7 Staying Fit to Swim

In general, swimming is easier on the body than most other sports. The low impact nature of swimming, combined with the reduced gravity environment, and the gentle resistance effect of the water make swimming statistically one of the lowest injury producing sports of all. Swimming is one of the few exercise routines that people can continue as long as they live, long after other athletic activities become impossible. In fact some swimmers, who have reached the point where walking is difficult, use a cane or walker to get to the edge of the pool, then once in the water, find the ease and efficiency of motion that they are no longer able to experience on land. Swimming is recognized as the best fitness activity for individuals with health limitations. It is frequently prescribed as therapy for conditions including arthritis, asthma and severe obesity. It is recommended as rehabilitation following back, hip and knee surgery. The positive effects of swimming greatly outweigh the risks.

However, there are some injuries and conditions that do show up among swimmers. It is important to note that not all of them are caused by swimming, but instead are sometimes existing conditions that are aggravated by swimming. Just the same, the key to preventing swimming-related injuries and worsening existing conditions is to understand their warning signs. When a sign occurs, do not ignore it. You are the only one your body sends these warning signals to. It is only you who can act accordingly. By being in touch with your body's signals, you are taking a major step in staying fit to swim, ensuring yourself lifelong participation and enjoyment of the sport.

7.1 UNDERSTANDING PAIN

People have different perceptions of physical pain. People's experience with pain also differs. Most people have experienced the pain of a headache, a toothache, or a minor burn. Some people have experienced the pain of a broken bone or a kidney stone. Despite our differences in perception and experience with physical pain, we understand it as a sign that something is wrong.

There are a few exceptions to the rule that pain means something is wrong. Childbirth, for instance has pain with it, but the result of this pain is positive: the birth of a baby. In most people's minds, athletics is another exception to this rule. In athletics, it is commonly accepted that a certain amount of pain is necessary to excel. Most of us grew up admiring athletes who had trained their bodies to a level that the average person could not reach. The very best athletes were seen as the ones who had the highest threshold for pain. They were able to work harder and become better than the average person who succumbed to the pain of pushing their bodies in higher athletic pursuit.

In reality though, athletic pain is more complex than many people realize. In fact, athletic pain must be understood as two distinct kinds of pain. Recognizing the difference is an essential part of being an athlete who continues to advance his or her performance, while remaining injury free.

The first kind of athletic pain is what most of us think of when we imagine what an accomplished athlete has gone through to attain his or her level of performance. It could be described as the sensation of being outside our comfort zone. We breathe hard, our heart beats fast, our muscles burn. Being able to endure this sort of discomfort, or pain associated with conditioning, is not harmful to a certain degree. It is "Okay Pain."

The second kind of pain is very important to distinguish from the first because it is an alarm that something is wrong. This kind of pain could be described as sharp or nagging. A distinct pain in a specific area of the body may occur when we do a certain action.

The pain may persist long after a workout. This is "Not Okay Pain." It should not be ignored. Willpower should not be used to endure it! "Swimming through" this kind of pain can result in a real injury that can keep a swimmer out of the pool for an extended period of time. If you experience "Not Okay Pain" while swimming, you should take action right away:

- Pinpoint the site of the pain in your body.
- Determine if there is any specific movement that makes it worse
- Tell these things to your coach immediately
- Modify your swimming to rest the affected area
- Take a day or two off if the pain persists

WHAT IS YOUR PAIN TELLING YOU?

7.2

Pain occurs most commonly in certain parts of swimmers' bodies, including the shoulders, knees and back. It is important for swimmers to understand what some of the possible causes for their pain are, to pay attention to it, and take appropriate action.

Shoulder Pain

SHOULDER INSTABILLITY

Shoulder instability is recognized as the single most important factor in causing pain and athletic injury to swimmers. The construction of the shoulder joint makes it very vulnerable in repetitive use sports, like swimming. The shoulder joint is shaped sort of like a golf tee, where it meets the bone of the upper arm. The bones do not lock together to stay in place. They are merely held in place by four small muscles surrounding the shoulder joint, called the rotator cuff, under the visible deltoid muscle of the shoulder.

Because swimmers tend to develop short muscles in their chest and long muscles in their back, the rotator cuff muscles around the shoulder joint can develop unevenly. When this happens, the bones are not held securely in place. The upper arm bone can fall slightly out of place, or worse, can move around at the shoulder joint, resulting in an unstable shoulder. Shoulder instability can lead to numerous other shoulder conditions, including bursitis and impingement syndrome, that should be recognized as symptoms of shoulder instability and treated accordingly. Shoulder instability in swimmers can be improved with specific exercises designed to strengthen the rotator cuff muscles. Many swimmers do these exercises routinely, even if shoulder pain is not a problem, as a preventive measure.

DRY LAND TRAINING

BURSITIS

Bursitis is the inflammation of the sack of fluid, called the bursa, which provides a cushion between the bones of the shoulder joint. It causes pain and soreness when the shoulder is used. Unfortunately, the pain of bursitis seems to be something that many swimmers can endure, leading them to "swim through it." Bursitis can be alleviated in a relatively short time if it is treated early with rest and ice. If ignored, it can become a chronic problem, which just gets worse. When the pain of bursitis subsides, attention should be turned to strengthening the rotator cuff to help prevent further another bout of bursitis.

DRY LAND TRAINING

IMPINGEMENT SYNDROME

Impingement Syndrome refers to the painful condition caused when the supraspinatus muscle that runs over the top of the shoulder is pinched between the bone of the upper arm and the point of the shoulder. This happens when the tissues around the shoulder joint are inflamed, preventing the muscle from moving smoothly between the bones as the arm is lifted. It is also aggravated by posture that allows the shoulders to drop toward the chest. Actively working to correct this posture problem, known as "swimmer's posture," by holding the shoulders back and moving the shoulder blades closer together in the back can sometimes help alleviate the pain of early shoulder impingement and help avoid further problems.

What Aggravates Shoulder Problems in the Water

- Incorrect swimming technique
- Overuse with poor technique
- Hand paddles

What Aggravates Shoulder Problems Out of the Water

- Walking a large dog
- Carrying a suitcase or groceries
- Holding a baby
- Opening sliding doors
- Ergonomically incorrect computer set up
- Vacuuming

What To Do

- Kick the rest of the workout or for several workouts
- Ice your shoulder
- Avoid out-of-the-water activities that cause pain
- See your doctor if the pain does not subside with rest
- Do shoulder stabilizing and strengthening exercises when you feel better
- Actively practice good posture

DRY LAND TRAINING

Knee Pain

MENISCUS DETERIORATION

The meniscus is the layer of cartilage that cushions the lower leg bones from the upper leg bone at the knee. Over a lifetime, this layer of cartilage can become thin, causing more impact between the upper and lower leg bones, which can be painful. The meniscus can also become frayed, causing irritation with movement, similar to a hang nail. Minor meniscal deterioration can cause on-again and off-again pain, that seems to appear and disappear for no apparent reason. Actual tears of the meniscus, or injuries where the meniscus becomes detached, are more common among land athletes, as there is more impact, twisting and pressure at the knee under the force of gravity, than in water. Still, the pain can manifest itself in the pool. A torn or detached meniscus may need to be corrected surgically.

WEAK HAMSTRINGS

Some knee pain is the result of underdeveloped muscles in the back of your upper leg, called hamstrings. This is seen most commonly in people beginning a program of running. This sort of knee pain is actually a protective mechanism of the body, to prevent the person from further activity that the leg muscles are not strong enough to do. The knees swell and activity becomes difficult and very painful. Swimmers who have just taken up running may feel this knee pain in the pool, as well. With rest, the swelling and pain subside, and activity can be resumed, starting very slowly and building up gradually. If ignored, this can be a chronic condition that will just get worse.

LIGAMENT DAMAGE

The upper and lower bones of the leg are joined at the knee by four ligaments that support the directional movement and leverage required of the legs. Strains and tears to the ligaments of the knee are common among land athletes but are rarely caused by swimming. Still, swimming activities can aggravate the pain of ligament damage. Modified swimming activities can sometimes be successful in avoiding pain, but stability to injured knee ligaments can only be fully restored with surgery.

What Aggravates Knee Problems in the Water

- Breaststroke kick
- Pushing off the wall
- Gripping a pull buoy
- Diving

What Aggravates Knee Problems Out of the Water

- Running
- Going up and down stairs
- Lateral movements
- Squatting

What To Do

- Avoid breaststroke kick and forceful push offs
- Ice your knee, front and back
- Elevate your knee if it is swollen
- Avoid out-of-the-water activities that cause pain
- See your doctor if the pain does not subside with rest
- Do leg strengthening exercises when you feel better

DRY LAND TRAINING

Back Pain

MUSKEL SPASMS

Muscle spasms of the lower back can cause debilitating pain. They often come without warning and can be relentless in their severity. Sometimes the pain is so severe, a person may go to the emergency room thinking something is wrong with one of their internal organs. Back spasms can occur as a result of a simple turn, lift or movement that a person has done before with no ill effects. The key to avoiding muscle spasms is to have well-developed muscles in both the back and the front of the body. This allows for a distribution of the work the body is being asked to do and lessens the chance that a single muscle will become strained by carrying an undue load.

For swimmers, the actions most frequently associated with muscle spasms in the back are butterfly and dolphin kick. Since the butterfly takes a great deal of strength and endurance to sustain, it is common for a swimmer's technique and timing to suffer if a lot of butterfly is done. Incorrect butterfly technique and timing can result in a great deal of strain on the back.

Pull buoys also can stress the muscles of the back by holding a swimmer's hips too high, resulting in a curved back. The muscles of the back strain as the swimmer attempts to straighten his or her posture against the pressure of the pull buoy. Using a smaller pull buoy can sometimes help. Some swimmers pull without a pull buoy, which is fine if the correct floatation can be maintained, otherwise avoiding pulling is a good idea. Strengthening the abdominal muscles to distribute the load is an excellent way to prevent back strain and painful muscle spasms.

DISK DEGENERATION

The bones of the spine, called vertebrae, have built-in shock absorbers between them, called disks. Natural degeneration and injury can cause these disks to bulge, rupture or slip and press against the many nerves around the spine. The pain associated with disk degeneration is chronic, and can become acute. The pain can affect the back and extend down the legs. It can sometimes only be alleviated by surgery to repair a damaged disk. Short of this drastic measure, doctors often recommend that patients with disk problems try to remain as active as possible. Swimming is frequently recommended because the pain of the condition is often alleviated by the reduced gravity environment of the water.

THIGHT HAMSTRINGS

Athletes with over-developed hamstring muscles sometimes suffer from back pain as the uneven muscle structure in their legs affects their posture and the way their trunk distributes a load. This phenomenon is frequently seen in runners who swim. Careful attention should be paid to the kicking technique of these individuals, as the tendency is to incorrectly power the kick with the hamstring muscles rather than the quadriceps in the front of the leg. Doing so will encourage ineffective kicking and worsen their back pain. A careful program of stretching is sometimes helpful for these individuals.

What Aggravates Back Pain In the Water

- Dolphin kick
- Butterfly
- Pull buoys
- Incorrect kicking

What Aggravates Back Pain Out of the Water

- Sitting for long periods of time
- Twisting
- Bending over
- Lifting

What To Do

- Avoid butterfly activities and using pull buoys
- Correct kicking technique
- Avoid out-of-the-water activities that cause pain
- See your doctor if the pain does not subside with rest
- Do back and abdominal strengthening exercises when you feel better

8 Swimming with Health Limitations

There are many health conditions that may limit swimming. This doesn't mean swimming cannot be enjoyed by a person living with a health limitation. Doctors frequently recommend swimming to people with certain conditions as the best way to maintain fitness without negatively affecting their health. By modifying swimming style, intensity and duration, swimming can provide many people with a sense of being less restricted by their health condition. Swimming is recommended by doctors for health conditions including:

ASTHMA

8.1

It is surprising how many Olympic swimming champions are asthmatics. Many of them began their swimming careers as children after their doctors prescribed swimming as a beneficial form of exercise for their condition. Asthma varies in severity and cause.

Reasons for its onset are not fully understood. When an asthma attack occurs, air flow is restricted due to the narrowing of the bronchial passages. The asthmatic may wheeze and cough in an attempt to restore normal breathing.

Some asthmatics are able to manage their condition through medication and by avoiding allergens. Doctors who encourage their asthmatic patients to swim often prescribe a portable, self-administered medication in the form of an inhaler that can be brought to the pool deck. By learning to monitor their symptoms during exercise, regulating swimming intensity, and using medication as indicated, many asthma sufferers can enjoy the benefits of swimming without anxiety.

8.2 ARTHRITIS

Arthritis is a painful condition that affects the joints causing stiffness, swelling, reduced range of motion and, in more advanced stages, weakness and deformity. Arthritis can affect the shoulders, elbows, wrists, fingers, hips, knees, and ankles among other joints and surrounding tissues.

There are many kinds of arthritis, and although the cause is unknown, many underlying conditions are associated with its onset, including injury, illness, and age. Many arthritis sufferers have found that some swimming actually alleviates their pain, as the mild compression effect of the water can reduce swelling and make movement less painful. Many doctors recommend swimming to arthritis sufferers to maintain range of motion.

8.3 MENOPAUSE

Menopause, or the time when ovulation stops, brings with it many physical and psychological changes to the lives of women. Although the average age to begin menopause is 51, many women experience symptoms as early as their 30s. Symptoms vary widely in frequency and severity. Physical symptoms can include hot flashes, weight gain, vaginal dryness and night sweats. Psychological symptoms can include depression, irritability, moodiness, loss of interest in sex, and inability to sleep. Psychological symptoms are attributed to diminishing estrogen levels consistent with menopause.

Although traditional treatments for menopausal symptoms include hormone replacement treatments, recent studies have uncovered risks associated with these therapies, including an increased chance of breast cancer and cardiovascular problems.

Many doctors are now recommending that women seeking relief from the symptoms of menopause take up a regular fitness routine. Researchers continue to show that exercise works as a mood elevator and as a hormone regulator. Many menopausal women who engage in regular exercise, such as Masters swimming, find their symptoms become less severe.

OSTEOPOROSIS

8.4

Osteoporosis, or the thinning of the bones, is a part of the aging process and present to some degree in all people of advanced age. However, it is most common in post-menopausal women, petite women, individuals who have had poor nutrition over many years, or those who have been inactive for a prolonged period of time.

Medical tests can determine if osteoporosis is present and to what degree. At its early stages, the progression of osteoporosis can be slowed with the help of exercise, which includes swimming in combination with weight-bearing activities.

Because swimming does not involve much weight-bearing activity, aside from pushing off the wall, other forms of exercise should be done that require the bones to bear weight. Walking is one of best ways to fend off osteoporosis. Still, swimming is often recommended as an activity for people with mild to moderate osteoporosis, because it provides the opportunity for a high degree of physical activity with a low risk of breaking fragile bones.

PREGNANCY

8.5

Pregnancy is by no means an illness, but nonetheless should be considered a limiting health condition when swimming. The physical demands of pregnancy, as well as the dramatic changes a woman's body goes through over a nine-month period require swimming activities to be modified as the pregnancy progresses. In conjunction with regular prenatal care, a pregnant swimmer can safely enjoy swimming throughout her term and benefit from continuing the activity.

The weightless environment of the water is the most comfortable place for many pregnant women to be! Swimming for exercise is also an excellent way to prepare for the strength and endurance required during labor. During each work out, the heart rate should be monitored several times. Most doctors recommend that a pregnant swimmer's activity should not make the heart rate exceed 120 beats per minute.

Some activities become uncomfortable to pregnant swimmers. These include flip turns, butterfly, and breaststroke kick. Still, there are plenty of activities that a pregnant woman can continue to do, allowing her to be comfortable and maintain the physical and social benefits of swimming.

CHAPTER 3
WORKING OUT

1 The Basics of Swimming Performance

Swimming performance is a complex sphere of numerous interlaced factors. At its most basic level, good swimming is best achieved by working at it from two sides: stroke mechanics, or technique, and physical fitness, or conditioning (Figure 3.1). Working toward good swimming from only one side will create improvement, but only to a certain extent.

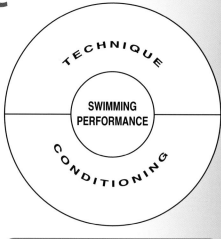

Figure 3.1

Swimmers can spend years working to improve their strokes by correcting and refining them, striving for the perfect stroke, but without a certain amount of conditioning work, they will not have the strength and endurance to sustain the stroke they have perfected for any distance. Likewise, swimmers can spend years working out, training with hard sets, improving their endurance and cardiovascular capabilities day after day, but without good stroke technique, they will not have the efficiency to make that conditioning work for them and achieve the most results. For this reason, good swimming is a matter that must be approached from two sides simultaneously. Swimmers should reach for their best swimming by working on their technique and conditioning. By doing so, swimmers will develop solid, efficient strokes and develop the ability to use those strokes over extended periods of swimming, making their workout time more productive and their improvement occur more rapidly.

2 The Fundamentals of Stroke Technique

Good stroke technique is necessary for good swimming. But what exactly does "good stroke technique" mean? Does it mean that excellent swimmers all swim exactly the same way? No. In fact, if you watched ten champions, swimming side by side, each swimmer's stroke would look different in many ways. So, what makes good stroke technique?

Basically, it is a matter of efficient forward motion. In comparing the strokes of those ten champions again, although each person's stroke is unique, there are fundamental ways in which they are the same. To achieve efficient forward motion, there are three skills that good swimmers all do well:

1. MINIMIZE DRAG

Minimizing drag means moving through the water with as little disruption as possible to that water. It means being aware of one's space in the water and working to make that profile smooth and compact. It means swimming like a fish swims, very streamlined and without much splashing (Figure 3.2). It means trying to slide forward through the water, instead of moving the water out of the way.

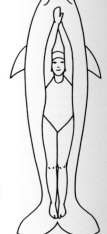

Figure 3.2 Minimize Drag

2. FEEL THE WATER

Feeling the water means that the swimmer learns to treat it as if it was more like a solid thing, rather than like air. It means using the water like a handle, as if the swimmer was rock climbing horizontally, advancing past that handle with each stroke (Figure 3.3). It means holding on to the water to create forward motion.

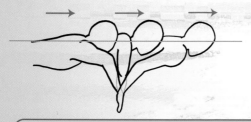

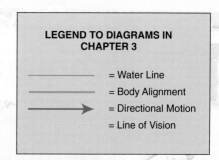

LEGEND TO DIAGRAMS IN CHAPTER 3

_____ = Water Line

_____ = Body Alignment

———————▶ = Directional Motion

_____ = Line of Vision

Figure 3.3   Feel the Water

3. ACCESS POTENTIAL POWER

Accessing potential power means that the swimmer uses the largest muscle groups available to accomplish forward motion, those being in the core, in combination with the muscles of the limbs (Figure 3.4). It means using the body's natural leverage to get the most out of each movement. It means that the swimmer learns to position his or her body and limbs most advantageously so that all available energy is spent moving the swimmer forward.

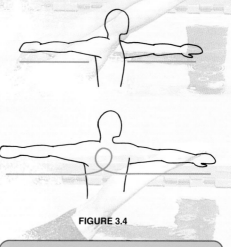

FIGURE 3.4

Figure 3.4   Access Potential Power

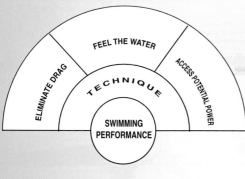

Figure 3.5

The "standard" of good stroke technique that we will concentrate on in this section is based on three fundamental points: minimizing drag, feeling the water and accessing potential power (Figure 3.5), in order to accomplish the goal of "efficient forward motion."

3 Analyzing Swimming Technique

While the specific form of each of the four competitive swimming strokes is different, there are common parts to each stroke, and the bottom line is that good stroke technique, or efficient swimming, requires the coordination or correct timing of all these parts:

3.1 BODY POSITION

The importance of body position in the water cannot be overstated. Body position, or how a swimmer lays on the water, affects his or her ability to achieve a streamlined path through the water, or swim instead unhindered by drag. A swimmer with poor body position will work much harder than a swimmer with a better floating position.

Body position affects the quality of the catch, or anchoring of the hands in the water. If a swimmer floats "uphill," with his feet much lower than his head, the catch will have to be used to correct floatation rather than to advance forward. Also, body position affects how much leverage is available to use, and therefore how much potential power can be accessed. Spending time developing good body position in the water is one of the very first steps to becoming a better swimmer.

3.2 ARM STROKE

The arm stroke can be looked at in three parts. First, the entry and catch, which extends and anchors the hands in the water, provides the swimmer with a point to advance beyond. Without a good catch, or ability to anchor the hands in the water, the rest of the arm stroke cannot produce effective forward motion. It is important to remember that the goal is to plant the hand in the water and move the body past that point, not to simply churn the arms through the water.

Second, there is the path of the pull, which encompasses the whole underwater portion of the stroke, through the point where the hand releases the water. During this phase of the stroke, some swimmers describe feeling a "pull," and then a "push," as their hand presses on the water. The "pull" is felt when the hand is in front of the shoulder, and then becomes a "push" as the hand passes by the shoulder towards the finish of the stroke. In trying to find this "pull" and "push," it is important to remember that it is really not just the arm that is "pulling" and "pushing," but it is the leverage from the core that must be employed to make this happen more effectively.

Finally, the third part of the stroke is the recovery, when the arm returns to the front for another stroke. The recovery should be relaxed but swift. It is the only phase of the stroke when the arms rest, so it is important to be able to generate the power for the recovery through leverage from the core.

KICK
3.3

The leg action in swimming serves several purposes. It provides a sort of rear motor that aids in momentum. It provides a balancing effect to the upper body motion. And it provides rhythm to the stroke. An effective kick can make a real difference in the quality of a swimmer's stroke productivity. Some people think that the kick should be used to keep the legs from sinking. Using the kick in this way takes more energy than it is worth and makes the other purposes of the kick secondary. The kick should help the swimmer go forward, not up.

BREATHING
3.4

In swimming, the act of timing one's inhalation and exhalation to the timing of the face being in or out of the water, and doing so without hindering the progress of the stroke, is a challenge that is not a part of other sports. In addition, in all strokes, the exhalation must be timed to the power phase of the stroke, and the inhalation timed to the recovery phase of the stroke for the most beneficial results. The most effective breathing in swimming is done by inhaling through the mouth and exhaling through the mouth and nose. This allows the most efficient exchange of new and old air, while preventing the uncomfortable feeling of water getting into the sinuses.

In the following sections, we will analyze each stroke in terms of its parts and then address the coordination of those parts. At the end of each stroke section is a "Troubleshooting" section designed to help solve common technique problems.

4 The Strokes

4.1 FREESTYLE

It is a common assertion that freestyle is the easiest stroke. Certainly, freestyle is the stroke that swimmers use most. It is not uncommon for a workout to be 80% or more freestyle. We warm up and cool down with freestyle. We use freestyle to time gauge our progress in distances from 50 yards to a mile or more. And because it is the stroke that most swimmers can go fastest with over a long distance, freestyle is what we use for open water swimming and for the swim leg of triathlons.

Historically, freestyle has been taught with the focus on what it looks like on top of the water. Special attention was given to elbow bend during recovery, the waterline at the head, and the amount of splash made by the kick. Today, coaches analyze freestyle in terms of what is going on under the water. It is now generally agreed that freestyle is the fastest stroke because it uses leverage most suited to the strength and balance of the human body. Although the underwater arm stroke is similar to that of butterfly, in the freestyle the arms alternate, allowing the stroke to produce continuous momentum,

making forward motion less strenuous than in the butterfly. And although the alternating arm motion of freestyle is similar to backstroke, in freestyle the arm stroke pulls underneath the body, which is a stronger pull position than the backstroke's pull down the side of the body.

With so many yards done in freestyle, many swimmers have developed the habit of swimming the stroke on "automatic pilot." And, while most swimmers have developed a highly conditioned freestyle, allowing this "cruise control" to work fairly well, freestyle technique is not given nearly as much attention as it should be, given how much the stroke is utilized. A common complaint about freestyle, more than any other stroke, is shoulder tightness and shoulder pain. "Freestyle shoulders" are most often attributed to overuse, and the solution given to many swimmers is to cut back, or even stop swimming. But looking more carefully, many cases of "freestyle shoulders" have another cause. Frequently, they stem from minor technique problems that are repeated over and over as swimmers use freestyle as the staple of their workouts. For this reason, freestyle technique should be a top and constant priority.

Body Position

Although at first glance it appears that the freestyle stroke is performed in a front floating position (thus the official name of the stroke, "front crawl"), this is a fundamental misunderstanding of the stroke. In fact, although the swimmer should look down at the bottom of the pool in freestyle, allowing the head to float in a neutral position, the rest of the body does not lie flat in the water at anytime during the stroke. The true floating position in freestyle is balancing on the armpit and the point of the hip bone (Figure 3.6).

This has been described by some as "swimming on your side," but this description is a bit misleading. Actually lying on your side in the water is as disadvantageous as lying flat. There is no leverage to speak of in either position. The correct position is in the middle of the two. This balance or float position is one extreme of the pendulum-like motion that the body makes in freestyle, from one armpit and hip to the other armpit and hip, never resting in the middle.

When a swimmer achieves the armpit-hip balance, it is very similar to the position a baseball batter takes before hitting the ball. It is also similar to a golfer just before he or she swings. Even a boxer finds this position when preparing to punch. For the human body, this is a position of strength, which gives most access for the next action to be powered by the core. For swimmers, that next action is to vault past the point where they have anchored their hand. It is very important to understand that this pendulum

Figure 3.6 Freestyle Roll

effect, or rolling action, is only half the story of correct body position in freestyle. The other half is that the swimmer must find a constant "downhill" position in order to swim most efficiently (Figure 3.7). This is achieved by pressing the breastbone down in the water, imagining it as the center point of the pendulum's swing. With the head at neutral, the swimmer looks downward toward the bottom of the pool, rather than straight ahead. Together, these two ways of lying or balancing in the water make the swimmer able to access the most power from the freestyle.

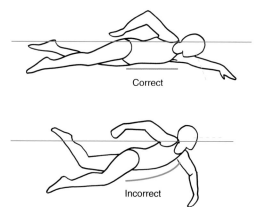

Correct

Incorrect

Figure 3.7 Freestyle Posture

Arm Stroke

The freestyle arm stroke has traditionally been taught as an "S" shaped pull. But presenting the arm stroke in this manner has often led swimmers to disassociate the pull from the core action, as they trace an "S" in the water with their hand when they swim. Perhaps a more precise description of what should occur is that as the body rolls from one extreme to the other, the path of the pull sweeps outward, inward, and then outward again, like an extended "S" (Figure 3.8). The fundamental distinction is that the path of the pull is a function of the body roll, not an independent action.

Figure 3.8   Path of Freestyle Arms Underwater

The arm stroke is made up of three parts: the extension and catch, the pull and release, and the recovery. The arm is able to reach full extension as the armpit and hip on the same side are at their lowest point, giving the swimmer the best position to make the "catch" by anchoring the forward reaching hand in the water. At this point, the extended hand should be aligned with, or even slightly outside the line of the armpit and hip (Figure 3.9). Simultaneously, the other arm is finishing its pull and preparing to release the water around the hip, as that side of the body rises to its highest point.

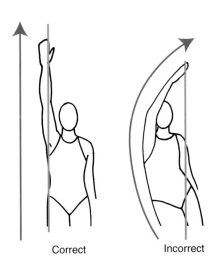

Correct   Incorrect

Figure 3.9   Freestyle Alignment

After the catch, the hand remains firmly anchored as the body advances forward. It is important here not to allow this long lever to lose power by collapsing or "dropping" your elbow (Figure 3.10). The elbow must stay high and firm throughout the arm pull. The wrist, as well, must not be allowed to collapse and should be held firm, although the hand changes pitch slightly throughout the path of the pull in order to maintain its hold on the water.

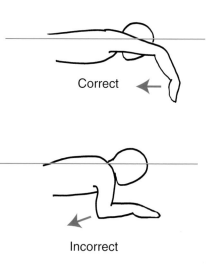

Correct

Incorrect

Figure 3.10 Underwater Elbow Position

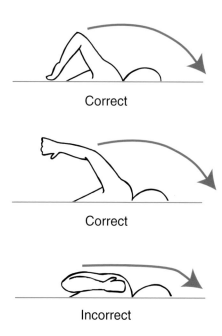

Correct

Correct

Incorrect

Figure 3.11 Recovery Elbow Position

The recovery of the freestyle is unique to every freestyler. While some swimmers have a 90-degree bend at the elbow, others recover with their arms almost straight. The fundamental similarity in the recoveries of all good freestylers is that they are relaxed. The recovery action is not generated from the hand pulling or leading the arm back to the front (Figure 3.11), but instead is generated from the body rolling from its highest position on that side, back to an armpit-and-hip-down position at the end of the recovery. By using the leverage of the core, the path of the elbow and hand during recovery should be higher than the shoulder.

Kick

Freestyle uses the flutter kick, an alternating kick that is unique to humans. While flutter kick can be extremely powerful, it also uses a disproportionate amount of the available energy a swimmer has, in light of how much forward motion it produces. It is commonly agreed that the kick in freestyle is only responsible for about 10 to 15 percent of a swimmer's speed, slightly more for sprinters. However, the kick in freestyle is still an essential part of the stroke because it provides lateral balance to the pendulum motion of the stroke, rhythm, as well as leverage to aide the firm anchoring of the hands in front.

Flutter kick is used in freestyle in a variety of rhythms. The most common rhythm is the 6-beat kick, which means that a swimmer kicks six times during each arm cycle of both arms. Other swimmers use four kicks per arm cycle. Some use 2 kicks per arm cycle, one kick per side of the pendulum, which often resembles a one legged dolphin kick. Still others use five or seven kicks per arm cycle, kicking more with one side of the pendulum than the other. Odd number kicking patterns are indicative of an asymmetrical stroke, which is not that uncommon in freestyle. The number of kicks per stroke that a swimmer does is often a function of the distance he or she is swimming. Generally, a quicker kicking rhythm, which produces more kicks, is used in sprinting, and a slower kicking rhythm, which produces fewer kicks, is used in longer distance swimming.

The flutter kick should be generated by the largest muscles in the leg, those in the thigh. In a whiplike motion, one leg drives downward, in a fluid motion, as if it had no bones. The foot is pointed, and slightly pigeon-toed, but also relaxed in order to get as much "flipper effect" as humanly possible. The depth of the kick should remain within the swimmer's profile. As one leg reaches its maximum depth, the other rises to the surface in a relaxed but straight position. The whole foot does not need to break the surface of the water for an effective kick. For most good kickers, the heel may break the surface, but the foot remains attached to the water. The splash that is present with the kick of fast freestylers is the result of water being displaced from underneath and moved quickly to the surface, rather than the result of the foot coming down from the air and making a hole in the water.

Breathing

Breathing must be an integral part of the stroke or it can break the leverage and rhythm of the freestyle. It must therefore be considered to be a function of the pendulum effect of the core, not an independent action. Breathing is done to the side, within the roll of the stroke. It is the only time the swimmer is not looking at the bottom of the pool.

Rather than turning his or her chin dramatically to get a breath, the swimmer's head follows the body's roll, for that stroke, to the point that the mouth has enough clearance to take in new air. If breathing to the right, the left temple, cheek and jawbone should remain in the water when inhaling. If breathing to the left, the right side of the face remains in the water. In either case, the chin remains aligned with the breastbone throughout the roll up and roll down of the breathing.

There is no one correct breathing pattern. Many swimmers breathe every other stroke, always on the same side. Many swimmers breathe on alternate sides, every three strokes. Alternate breathing is considered a good way to encourage a very symmetrical roll. Some swimmers breathe every four, every six or more strokes. Infrequent breathing is most commonly seen in freestyle sprinting since it is sustainable only for a short time.

Coordination

Coordinating the arms, the legs and the breathing to work with the body roll is essential for an efficient, sustainable, and shoulder-saving freestyle. In freestyle, the arm action is not uniform in speed. More time is spent with the arms toward the front, creating a sort of "catch up" timing. Although there is a point in the stroke where the arms are opposite, the recovering arm catches up with the anchoring arm in the later part of the stroke, and the recovery is quicker than the initial stage of the stroke.

The timing of the breathing to the arms should be focused on during both the inhalation and the exhalation. The inhalation to the side should occur when opposite side hand extends in front. If the inhalation occurs later than this, there is a temptation to press down on the water to get your face clear to breathe. It is important to continue the forward line of the stroke while breathing by reaching forward, not down (Figure 3.12). The exhalation should be timed to begin with the anchoring of the other arm and continue to the end of the pull.

The timing of the kick varies by the number of kicks a swimmer does with each arm cycle. However, a dominant kick should be timed to happen simultaneously with the arm extension and catch for the best coordination.

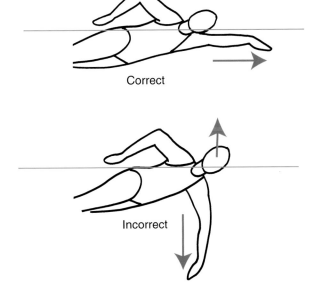

Correct

Incorrect

Figure 3.12   Freestyle Breathing

Troubleshooting Freestyle

I don't feel a catch when my hand extends in the front.

ARM STROKE You might be trying to catch water before your arm is completely extended. Doing this shortens the lever of the stroke and makes your hand hurry to the back of the pull, leaving no opportunity to catch water.

You might be over-reaching. This means your hands are entering more aligned to your nose than to your shoulder. Doing this means you lose the leverage that a shoulder-width entry produces. It also knocks off the alignment of your body position, forcing you to use your stroke to correct your direction, rather than to move you forward.

BODY POSITION You also might be swimming too flat. When you swim flat, you don't get the extension you need for a great catch, and you don't have the strength of your core to help, you only have your arms.

I can't seem to clear the water in order to breathe.

Often this is a timing issue. You might be trying to turn your head by itself without the assistance of the natural rotation of the stroke. You could also be starting your breathing too late in the stroke, when your hand has already left the front, causing you to sink when you *COORDINATION* are trying to breathe. In either case, slow down and time the inhalation to the beginning of the opposite side arm stroke, and the exhalation to finish with the arm stroke your face is turning toward.

I can't seem to release the water at the end of the stroke.

It could be that you have collapsed your elbow during the stroke. If this happens, your elbow will be finishing the stroke before your hand, and your hand will get stuck in the water. Remember to keep your elbow high and firm during the arm stroke so the hand passes it and finishes the stroke first.

It could also be that your hand is leading your recovery. If your hand pulls the rest of the arm forward, the elbow usually drops down, sometimes low enough to drag through the water. Hold your hand loose and practice allowing the rotation of the stroke generate your recovery. It should feel like your arm is being thrown forward.

ARM STROKE

I get shoulder pain when I do my freestyle recovery.

This is an indication that your recovery is not a function of your rotation. You might be swimming too flat and putting a lot of stress on the shoulder joint as you lift your arm up to clear the water to recover.

Also, it could be that your hand is leading your recovery. This usually makes for a low elbow recovery. In this position, the shoulder joint does not move freely.

BODY POSITION

It could also be an effect of over-reaching. When the recovery ends too far toward the center, aligning with the nose rather than the shoulder, it results in more torque on the shoulder joint than necessary.

ARM STROKE

I get shoulder pain during my freestyle pull.

If you get pain early in the pull, it could be a result of over-reaching. When you are aligned too far to the center, you have to pull laterally outward before making any forward progress. This lateral movement is not easy on the shoulder.

ARM STROKE

If you get pain later in your stroke, it could be that your pulling arm is too straight in the mid pull. If the hand is too far away from your body during the middle of the pull, you have less leverage than if your hand is close. This is well illustrated by trying to pull yourself out of the water in two ways: first with straight arms then again with arms bent at the elbows. Which is easier? Pulling with the hands closer to your body in the middle of the action is easier.

It also could be that you are pulling past the centerline of your body. If you over-reach in this way, you again put undue stress on the shoulder.

4.2 BACKSTROKE

It is safe to say that backstroke is the least popular stroke. There are many reasons swimmers cite for not enjoying backstroke. Most commonly, swimmers say that it makes them nervous to swim upside down without being able to see where they are going. There is a lot to bump into in a pool, after all! Further, swimmers don't like water in their nose. Nose clips are more frequently used by swimmers doing backstroke than any other stroke. Lastly, backstroke makes a lot of swimmers tired. Backstroke seems to take more effort than the other strokes do because the power phase of the kick is done in an upward direction, against gravity.

For the most part, backstroke is a very misunderstood stroke. Common myths about backstroke include: that it uses a windmill type arm action, that you need to arch your back to do backstroke, that the back of your head stays out of the water, that you kick the water downward for the most power, and that only one arm moves at a time. Each of these myths contributes to its own technique problem to one degree or another. Whether it is because many swimmers are self-taught backstrokers, simulating what they have seen other swimmers do, or because they have just been taught incorrectly, misconceptions about backstroke are very common.

They are the root of backstroke dislike, and can even lead to shoulder problems, if not addressed early. Done right, backstroke can be a very relaxing, balanced stroke, which gives swimmers a welcome break from looking at the bottom of the pool.

Body Position

The correct floating position for backstroke is with the face above the water, but the ears under the water, and the hips held near the surface by a tight core and a straight spine. To access core strength in backstroke, it is necessary to keep the spine as straight as possible. This is contrary to the common urge to arch the back in order to correct floating problems, in an attempt to stay on the surface (Figure 3.13).

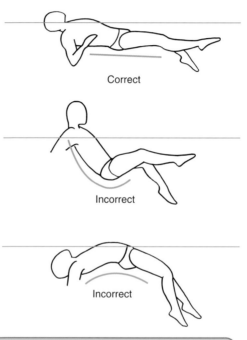

Correct

Incorrect

Incorrect

Figure 3.13   Backstroke Posture

By arching the back, a swimmer's face usually ends up submerged to some extent, and the feet are low in the water. The direction that the swimmer then aims becomes downward rather than forward. Keeping the spine as straight as possible aligns the motion forward. It also gives swimmers an axis to swim from and a good fulcrum for the lever of their core.

A swimmer can practice this alignment by standing with his or her back to a wall and working to press every part of the spine into the wall, from the head to the hips. Notice that when this is accomplished, the abdominal muscles are slightly contracted, and

the pelvis is tilted forward a bit, holding the position firm.

The leverage in backstroke, comes from a rolling action, where the body turns on the firm axis of the spine from side to side, supplying power to the arm stroke. (Figure 3.14) Without this rolling action, the potential power of the stroke is dramatically reduced.

Figure 3.14 Backstroke Roll

Arm Stroke

Backstroke is known as an opposition stroke, which means that when one arm is up, the other is down, and when one arm is in the water, the other is out. Both arms move continuously. Some swimmers understand this as a windmill action, which is true only in part. It is also only partly true that the backstroke arms are always opposite. To clarify: the backstroker's hand enters the water, pinkie first over the head, in line with the shoulder (Figure 3.15), and anchors it just below the surface about the same depth as the width from breastbone to shoulder. It is at the point, that the other arm exits the water, the hand near the thigh.

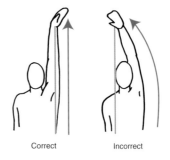

Correct   Incorrect

Figure 3.15 Backstroke Hand Entry

So, there is an instant when both hands are in the water, one over the head and the other at the side … not quite opposite. The path of the anchored arm is along the side of the body (Figure 3.16), elbow bent but firm, as if throwing a ball at your feet, not below the body's

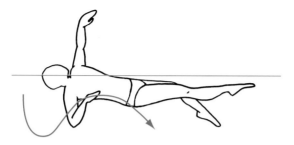

Figure 3.16   Path of Backstroke Arms Underwater

Figure 3.17   Incorrect Windmill Action

profile in a circular or windmill motion at all (Figure 3.17). As the anchored arm is pulling, the other arm is recovering in a straight arm motion, which does resemble a windmill, elbow locked, and hands pitched outward at the wrist. At the middle point of the recovery, the arms are truly opposite of each other but are not a mirror image of each other. The rolling action of the body is crucial in developing an effective arm stroke. Without a roll, the hand cannot anchor properly, and the available leverage cannot be accessed. In addition, without rolling, the other hand cannot exit the water without creating quite a bit of drag. Because the arm stroke ends below the surface of the water, it is necessary to roll the hip up, to bring the arm near the thigh back up to the surface to begin the recovery properly. At the midpoint of the recovery, when the arm is exactly perpendicular to the body, the entire armpit of that arm should be out of the water. Likewise, the armpit of the other arm should be at its deepest point.

Kick

Like freestyle, the backstroke uses the flutter kick, which works in an alternating fashion, so that when one foot reaches the top of the motion, the other is at its deepest point.

Good backstrokers have extremely flexible ankles and can easily point their toes, creating a straight line from the knee to the big toe. Some swimmers can do this easier than others. But one thing all swimmers can do is to position their feet in a pigeon-toed position. Like very pointed toes, this position produces more foot surface with which to kick the water.

In backstroke, the main thrust of the kick should be an upward motion (Figure 3.18). The heel should be dropped down below the surface of the water but still be within the profile of the stroke. Then the top of the foot should be forced upward quickly, as if trying to kick a ball floating on the surface of the water. This kind of kick should create a boiling effect on the water's surface, which happens as the foot moves deep water rapidly toward the surface. This boil, or splash, is created even without the foot breaking the water's surface.

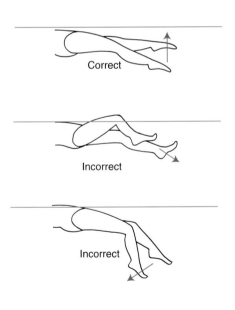

It is important to remember that the knees, too, should not break the surface in backstroke, or the kick will produce more drag than forward motion. To maintain a streamlined position while kicking, avoid bending at the hips to kick and lifting the knees as if bicycling or marching.

Figure 3.18 Backstroke Kick

Breathing

Most people discount breathing as an issue in backstroke because the swimmer's face is out of the water. In fact, breathing is very important to maintaining the rhythm of the stroke. The most common breathing pattern is to choose an inhalation arm, and an exhalation arm. When the armpit of the inhalation arm is at its highest, it creates a sort of barrier to the water. This is the time to inhale. Then, when the exhalation arm is pulling, exhale completely.

It is very important not to hold your breath in backstroke, although it is tempting. The exchange of old air for new air is essential in being able to perform the stroke over any distance. This is true for any physical activity. For example, how long would you last running if you held your breath?

Coordination

Most good backstrokers use about six kicks for every complete arm cycle, that is both arms going around once. That means the legs are moving about three times as fast as the arms. The head remains still on its axis while the arms turn, powered by the core that is rolling into and out of each stroke.

The kick is best coordinated by timing the power phase, or upbeat of a dominant kick to the moment that the hand is anchored, in an "X"-type balance: left arm anchoring when the right foot is kicking up.

Many good backstokers believe that the key to good backstroke is fitting the stroke into the breathing rhythm, rather than fitting the breathing into the stroke rhythm. Maintaining an even and relaxed breathing rhythm gives the stroke a good sustainable cadence.

Troubleshooting Backstroke

It's impossible to go straight.

ARM STROKE

It is hard but not impossible. Often, a very small stroke flaw can appear huge because each stroke sets you further and further off course. It takes concentration, and it takes awareness of the hand entry that you cannot see. In this stroke, you just have to "know" where your hand is entering the water. It should enter directly in line with your shoulder, not behind your head.

This is something that you can practice in the mirror at home: Close your eyes and raise your hand to full extension like in backstroke at the end of the recovery. Now open your eyes. Is your hand aligned with your shoulder? Make adjustments with your eyes closed and then check it in the mirror until you know you are aligned. In the water, practice during uncrowded times, if you are concerned about colliding with other swimmers. It really does get better with practice.

I get water in my face all the time.

BODY POSITION

KICK

Believe it or not, good backstrokers have water in their face most of the time. You just have to get to know the rhythm of the waves going over your face. Learn to time your inhale to the moment when your face is clear, then exhale from both nose and mouth when the water is over your face. If you develop a good roll, the shoulder that is high will actually create a brief barrier to the water in your face, leaving you the perfect opportunity to inhale.

It hurts my shoulders.

ARM STROKE

Backstroke can be hard on the shoulder joints if the stroke is done as one big circle, or windmill action, as many of us were taught. If you think about that circle, from the deepest point back up around to the surface, you are actually pulling yourself underwater instead of moving yourself forward! A more efficient and shoulder-saving stroke path is down the side of the body, with the elbow bent but firm at mid pull, sort of like you are throwing a ball at your feet.

I get out of breath.

Many swimmers believe that since they are not face down in the water, breathing is not a concern in backstroke. The fact is, just as in all strokes, a consistent breathing pattern is essential to sustaining the activity. Swimmers sometimes just hold their breath in backstroke until they absolutely have to take a breath. Try instead a breathing pattern where you inhale on one arm, exhale on the other. Also, make sure you are inhaling deeply and exhaling fully each time.

BACKSTROKE BREATHING

I sink.

It might be your kick, but more likely it is a body position problem that is making you sink. First and foremost, your ears should be underwater the whole time in backstroke. Holding your head up to keep water out of your ears will make your hips and legs sink. Remember, the more forward motion you produce, the more water will go by your ears, rather than into them. Second, tighten your abdominal muscles, rocking your pelvis forward, then squeeze your butt like you are holding a coin between your cheeks. Now swim without dropping it! As far as your kick, position your feet pigeon-toed. Push the water with the tops of your feet in small quick, upward kicks. Try to relax and let the water hold you.

BODY POSITION

KICK

4.3 BUTTERFLY

Done right, the butterfly is an awesome sight that blends immense power, rhythm and grace. The newest of the four competitive strokes, the butterfly, was developed in the 1940s, as swimmers experimented with how to make the breaststroke faster. Originally, it was called the dolphin breaststroke. In fact, in Masters swimming, using a butterfly arm stroke with a breaststroke kick is still legal, although for most swimmers, it is not the fastest alternative. The butterfly stroke was finally included in the rulebook as an official stroke, in its own right, in the 1950s. Because of its relatively new status, evolution in butterfly technique is ongoing. The butterfly we have watched Olympians do, and that many of us learned as youth swimmers, with it's "keyhole" pull and arm stroke pulling down to the hips, has evolved into an even more powerful stroke.

Today, swimmers are taught the "Y" butterfly, which, although similar to the traditional butterfly in many ways, takes much of the emphasis off the arm stroke and places it more on the core. Swimmers just learning the butterfly have found this stroke easier to learn than the old style. Veteran butterflyers, too, are encouraged to try this new stroke...You CAN teach an old dog new tricks! Done right, this new butterfly is less exhausting and sustainable over a longer distance by depending more on the large muscles of the trunk and less on the smaller muscles of the limbs.

Body Position

Because butterfly is a symmetrical stroke and both sides of the body operate in simultaneous motion, a rocking, or tipping, motion is used to achieve leverage (Figure 3.19).

The swimmer shifts his or her weight subtly but rhythmically forward and back, so the most leverage is gained from each stroke. Without this shift of weight, the butterfly loses much of its leverage, leaving the swimmer with only the power of the arms and legs (Figure 3.20).

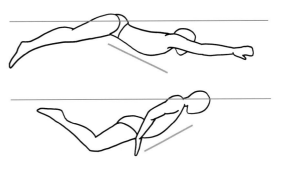

Figure 3.19   Butterfly Tripping Motion

Now, it is a fact that swimming, like most physical activity, is easier done in a "downhill" position than an "uphill" position. It is therefore important to remember that, although it is necessary to have a tip both forward and back in the butterfly, the majority of a swimmer's effort should be focused on getting back to the "downhill" position. This position, with the chest low and hips high, keeps the forward momentum of the stroke going.

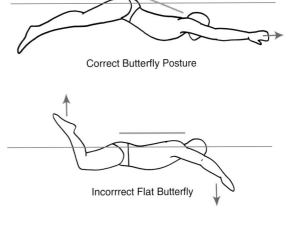

Correct Butterfly Posture

Incorrrect Flat Butterfly

Figure 3.20

Arm Stroke

The entry position of the arms in the butterfly is in a wide "Y" slightly outside the shoulders, with the arms extended in order to anchor the hands firmly just below the surface of the water. Hands are best positioned at an outward pitch, continuing the line of the "Y", with the thumbs slightly lower than the little fingers (Figure 3.21).

Correct   Incorrect

The path of the arm stroke is round, starting with the hands outside the shoulders and sweeping inward under the chest, then outward around the bellybutton to finish the stroke, release the water and begin the arm stroke recovery (Figure 3.22).

Figure 3.21 Butterfly Armstroke Entry

Although the arms do bend at the elbows during the middle phase of the pull, as the hands pass closer to the swimmer's belly, it is important to remember not to allow the elbows to drop down or the leverage in the arm action will be lost. With the elbow high and firm, the swimmer's hands can maintain their handle on the water. When the hands release the water at the end of the pull, they should exit the water with the little finger first. They should remain in that position for as long as possible during recovery, in order to allow the arms to relax, or recover, and to maximize the momentum carried forward from stroke to stroke. Recovering in this position also avoids the elbows dragging through the water.

Figure 3.22 Path of Butterfly Arms Underwater

Kick

The dolphin kick used in the butterfly is more than a leg action. It is a full body action, and so, it would be more accurately described as a "dolphin action" rather than a kick (Figure 3.23). When learning the dolphin, it is a very good idea to observe fish. Their dolphin action is fluid, like a wave, and is not a big motion, with a lot of effort or splashing. Their dolphin is a very integrated action that is initiated in the "core," and is transferred in a whiplike action to the tail. Notice, that fish do not have knees, hips, waist, or a neck that would break the whip action of the dolphin. If you study a fish swimming, notice how it is so fluid that it appears as if it has no bones. This is how we, as humans, must approach the dolphin, like fish do. After all, they are the experts.

Two kicks occur during each butterfly stroke. The first kick sends the swimmer forward and slightly downward with the beginning of the arm stroke, and the second kick sends the swimmer forward and slightly upward with the end of the arm stroke.

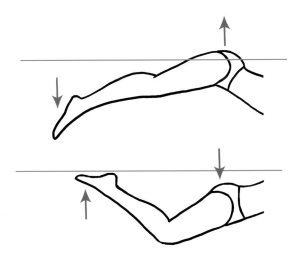

Figure 3.23   Dolphin Action

Breathing

Breathing in butterfly must be done within the line of the stroke, or it can work like putting on the brakes. Breathing is best done forward, neck extended like a turtle coming out of his shell, in order to continue the forward momentum of the stroke (Figure 3.24).

Allow very little clearance from the water, by keeping the chin on the surface of the water. This avoids lifting oneself too high so the tipping motion of the stroke becomes out of balance and an "uphill" butterfly occurs. Looking down at the water, while breathing, rather than at the wall in front ahead will keep the head within the line of the stroke. The face clears the water to breathe during the first part of the pull, as the chest rises. The face returns to the water an instant before the hands reach the wide "Y" at the end of the recovery.

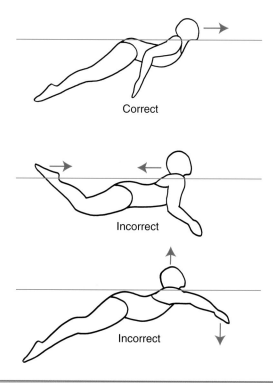

Correct

Incorrect

Incorrect

Figure 3.24 Timing of Butterfly Breathing

Coordination

Butterfly works on leverage. The arms enter the water in front of the swimmer as a wide "Y", outside of the shoulders while the head stays firmly in a neutral position. When in this position, the swimmer presses downward on the water with the chest, shifting his or her weight as far forward as possible. As the chest presses downward, the hips rise, producing a "riding downhill" feeling.

In the wide "Y" arm position, with the chest low and hips high, the swimmer is able to anchor the hands in the water, then vault his or her body forward past the hands, by sliding the hips down and forward toward the anchored hands.

The arm stroke becomes short and quick, and the kick actually becomes a consequence of the chest and hip-tipping movement, not an independent action. The first kick is achieved when the hands are in front of the swimmer in the wide "Y". The action of pressing the chest down and letting the hips rise up creates a lever-like action that whips down to the feet, thus resulting in a kick.

The second kick is achieved as the swimmer finishes vaulting past the hands, at the end of the breath, with another whiplike action that extends to the feet. At this point, the swimmer has shifted his or her weight back toward the hips. As the recovery begins, once again, the swimmer shifts his or her weight forward.

Troubleshooting Butterfly

My butterfly only has one kick.

COORDINATION & KICK

A single kick during each butterfly stroke is usually a timing issue. Slow down. Focus on timing the downbeat of the first kick with your arm entry and the downbeat of your second kick to the finish before the arm stroke moves to the recovery phase.

Remember that the kick is part of the entire body motion, which tips forward and back, and extends to the feet. Make sure you are not initiating your kick by bending your knees, causing you to just use your feet and lower legs to kick. Doing so flattens out your butterfly too much. Your hips and abdominal muscles must be involved in the kick to maintain the tipping action and leverage of the stroke.

KICK

You may also be kicking too deep. With a deep kick, the legs will take too long to come back to their original position and the arms may have already finished their stroke, thus leaving no opportunity to fit the second kick into the stroke.

I can't get my arms over the water for recovery.

ARM STROKE

You may be using too long a pull, resulting in the arms getting stuck in the water at the end of the stroke. If you hold onto the water too long, in effect what happens is that you lift water up and pull yourself down, lower, into the water. Try finishing your arm stroke by sweeping slightly out to the side. Doing so should help your hands release the water better.

KICK & COORDINATION

Your second kick may also be too early. The downbeat of the second kick plays an important role in giving you the lift and power to get your arms back to the front. It should occur with the finish of the underwater arm stroke, before the recovery begins. Hold the second kick until that point. It could also be that you may be recovering with your elbows down, so that they drag through the water, working against the forward momentum of the stroke. You can easily fix this by recovering with your hands in a "pinkie up" position. This creates a sort of an arch over the water with your arms.

I can only keep my stroke rhythm if I don't breathe.

You might be lifting yourself too high over the water to breathe. Doing so will knock your timing off and change the direction of your stroke from forward, which is what you want, to up and down.

BODY POSITION

It could be that you are starting to breathe too late in the stroke. By beginning the breathing process when your underwater arm stroke is almost finished, the leverage action of your stroke is broken, and it becomes difficult to get your face out to breathe. Your face should clear the water to breathe after you anchor your hands, as your chest rises, and the inhalation should finished by about the middle of the recovery.

BREATHING

Butterfly hurts my back.

You might be kicking up when you are breathing. In doing so, your back takes a lot of pressure. Remember that when your face is up to breathe, you should be in a slight "uphill position," meaning that your feet should be at their lowest point, having just kicked down, while your face is at its highest point, for the breath.

COORDINATION

Butterfly takes a great deal of abdominal strength and, without it, your back may try to compensate. Try strengthening your core with by doing crunches and other abdominal exercises.

DRY LAND TRAINING

My kick doesn't have any power.

A kick that doesn't produce much power, or forward motion, usually happens when the kick stops at the knee. Instead of lifting the heels up to kick, which makes you bend your knees too much, try dropping your knees down just slightly, leaving your hips and your feet aligned high, and then raise your hips as you let your feet snap downward. After you have achieved this much more powerful kind of kick, try incorporating your core muscles into the hip action, for even more power.

KICK

4.4 BREASTSTROKE

Breaststroke has changed more than any other stroke over the past few decades. Many Masters swimmers who competed as children remember the rules of breaststroke meant that it had to be performed very carefully: The top of a swimmer's head had to stay out of the water at all times, the arm stroke had to be completely underwater, and the hips remained motionless. Swimmers struggled to achieve speed with these limitations, experimenting with extremely wide kicks and huge arm circles to move themselves forward. Changes in the official rules for breaststroke have eliminated these restrictions. Swimmers and coaches have developed ways to access more leverage, and to minimize the drag that is an inherent problem in the stroke. Breaststroke has become more efficient and faster. In fact, breaststroke records across the board have increased dramatically since the new rules have been adopted.

Basically, the new breaststroke allows swimmers to depart from the flat swimming style that many of us were taught as kids and use a motion similar to the butterfly tipping motion to power the stroke. This has led to an almost universal practice of breathing with every stroke, which is also different than years past. There is also less of a

glide phase in the newer stroke, as swimmers work to accelerate the rate of the stroke. Some swimmers have developed an arm stroke recovery that is completely out of the water, working from the theory that by doing so the arms create less drag. Others rely on a partial over-the-water recovery that they believe saves energy but still improves the speed with which the arms return to the front.

Some things have remained the same about the breaststroke. Both the arms and the legs are still moved in a symmetrical motion. The feet still must remain underwater, and the sequence of the stroke is still the same: "pull, breathe, kick, glide." In essence, breaststroke is no longer a relaxed, resting type of stroke. It has become a power stroke that requires a great deal of technical perfection and precise timing. That being said, breaststroke remains the stroke with the most variations.

Body Position

Breaststroke is unique in that the stroke, for the most part, happens underwater. In addition, it is the only stroke in which the kick extends outside the profile of the body. The arm stroke, too, is unique, in that it is shorter than other strokes, extending only to the chest. For these reasons, a streamlined body position is important to perfect. With actual drag being greater than in all other strokes, any opportunity to move through the water in a more streamlined position should be maximized. The main opportunity in the breaststroke to do 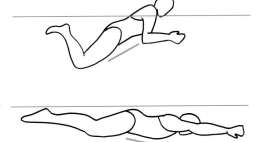 this is during the glide phase of the stroke, which occurs as the kick finishes and the arms have already reached the front and the face is in the water. Though the length of the glide is extremely variable from breaststroker to breaststroker, the bottom line is that this phase of

Figure 3.25   Breaststroke Tipping Motion

the stroke should be held for as long as it is productive in order to benefit from the power and forward motion of the previous stroke. Gliding slightly "downhill" is the position breaststrokers strive for.

As in butterfly, a rocking, or tipping motion is used while the swimmer performs the symmetrical arm stroke and kick (Figure 3.25). The degree of this tipping varies greatly from swimmer to swimmer, but the essential practice of shifting one's weight forward and back is the way leverage is applied to each stroke. By using a tipping motion in breaststroke, which is powered by the leverage in the core, the swimmer pulls himself or herself up and forward to breathe, and kicks himself or herself down and forward to glide.

Arm Stroke

The arm stroke in breaststroke produces the least forward motion of any of the four competitive strokes. It takes a shorter, and more lateral path than the other strokes. Some swimmers compare the breaststroke arm stroke to sculling more than pulling. From the starting point of extended arms and hands held together in a point (Figure 3.26), the hands press outward, to a wide "Y" position similar to the butterfly. The hands anchor slightly outside the line of the shoulders, just below the surface

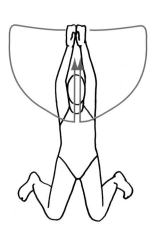

of the water. At this point, the hands are pitched outward, thumbs downward. From there, the hands change their pitch to a thumbs-up position as the path of the pull, or skull, changes directions and presses inward, slightly toward the chest. The swimmer strives to hold on to the same water the whole time. During this inward sweep the elbows are held high and firm for the most leverage. As the hands come together in front of the chest, the elbows fold in toward the ribs, the water is released, and the recovery begins.

Figure 3.26 Path of Breaststroke Arms Underwater

Swimmers recover their arms in a variety of positions. Some begin the recovery with their hands together and pointed, and shoot them forward into streamline. Others recover with their palms together and then shift to a palms-down position upon full extension. Where the arms are in relation to the water during recovery also varies widely. Some swimmers recover their arms entirely over the water, in order to minimize the drag of an underwater recovery. This requires a great deal of upper body strength, as these swimmers must get their bodies higher out of the water to achieve it. Some swimmers start their recovery with their hands out of the water, then dive them down and forward in order to increase the momentum of the "downhill" glide. Others recover with their hands submerged completely, in a less dramatic, but tried and true fashion. Despite the variations in recovery style, it is agreed that the recovery should be done quickly, in order to get back to streamline and into the starting position for another stroke. The breaststroke recovery should appear as if the swimmer is threading a needle with his or her hands, elbows, shoulders and head, chest, hips, legs and finally the feet.

Kick

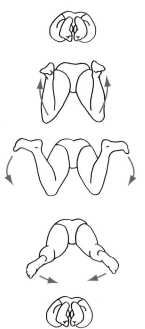

Breaststroke is the only stroke in which the kick produces more power than the arms. The breaststroke kick is the most technically complex kick, requiring the feet to go from maximum flex to maximum point during each kick (Figure 3.27). Three sets of joints are involved in the breaststroke kick: those in the hips, knees, and ankles. Of these three, the hip joints move the least. This seems contrary to what seems to be happening when observing the breaststroke kick, with its frog-like retraction of the legs, and the circular path that the kick takes. In reality, the hips bend just slightly, as the legs prepare to kick. During the actual kick, the

Figure 3.27   Path of Breaststroke Kick

hips hold firm until the very end. This allows more water to pass by the swimmer, instead of bumping into him or her, producing drag (Figure 3.28).

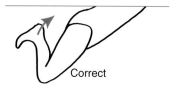

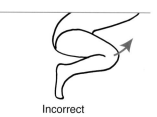

The bend of the knees is more significant, as the swimmer draws the heels back toward the hips as far as possible, with the knees opening about shoulder width apart, or at least wider apart than the heels (Figure 3.29).

Figure 3.28 Lift Ankles, Not Knees

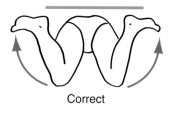

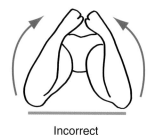

The knees stay firmly at that width until the end of the kick. While the knees are held firmly, the lower part of the legs can rotate from the fixed position of the knees, sweeping outward then back, and finally inward, getting the most power out of the kick.

Finally, as the heels are brought upward, the feet are flexed at the ankles into a position so that the soles of the feet are flat just under the surface of the water (Figure 3.30), turned outward as much as possible

Figure 3.29 Position Feet Outside Knees

and positioned farther apart than the knees. It is the ankles that are key to the breaststroke. As the power phase of the kick begins, the soles of the feet, pointing out and flexed, press the water outward and back away from the hips. Some breaststrokers say that they also push the water with the inside of their ankles and lower legs at this

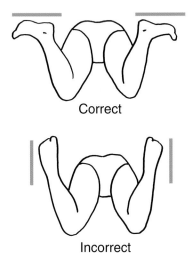

Correct

Incorrect

Figure 3.30   Flex Feet

point in the kick. Still pressing on the same water, as the kick gains speed, the path of the kick then begins to sweep inward, and the feet, though still flexed, change pitch slightly to maintain their hold on the water. Finally, as the legs near the finish of the kick, the knees are brought back together into streamline as the ankles sweep the feet into the toes pointed position with a final thrust. The ankle flexibility of some breaststrokers is so great that they are able to finish their kick by clapping the soles of their feet together. Simultaneously, the legs lift, so the feet finish slightly higher than the hips, preparing for the "downhill" glide.

Breathing

The breathing in breaststroke is possible through the natural lever effect of the stroke. It is therefore not necessary to raise the chin to clear the face from the water to inhale or to lower the chin to return the face back into the water. In fact, "nodding," or altering, the chin position actually breaks the lever of the stroke.

The breathing should happen when the chest is at its highest point and the hips are at their lowest. Keeping the head firmly in the line of the stroke, the swimmer should be looking down at the water (Figure 3.31), not at the other end of the pool when inhaling. By holding the head firm, the breathing action does not interrupt the forward line of the stroke, as it easily can with a "nodding" type breathing technique, where the chin leads the body up and down rather than forward. The amount each swimmer's face clears the water when breathing varies widely.

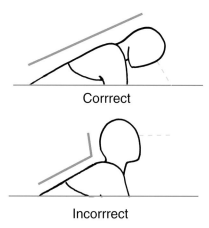

Corrrect

Incorrrect

Figure 3.31 Breaststroke Breathing Alignment

Coordination

Probably more than any other stroke, timing is a crucial factor in breaststroke. If the power movements of the breaststroke are timed incorrectly, the innate periods of drag in the stroke can actually cancel each other out (Figure 3.32). The correct sequence of the breaststroke is "pull, breathe, kick, glide." Some swimmers have distilled this four-part sequence into two actions: "pull and breathe, then kick and glide." However, the sequence remains the same.

While, unlike the other strokes, it is the kick that produces the most power in the breaststroke, the kick does not work in isolation. It is connected in essence to other actions of the stroke. For instance, breathing in breaststroke serves two purposes. First, of course, it gives the swimmer an opportunity to get new air. Second, in the breathing position, the body is tipped back, head high and hips low, allowing the most water to cover the feet at the point when they are drawn up to their maximum bend toward the hips, in preparation to kick.

The arm stroke and breathing are closely timed to finish and return to streamline just before the kick finishes. This allows the maximum forward motion to be achieved from the kick, while the potential drag of the arm stroke recovery and the "uphill" position of the breathing is minimized.

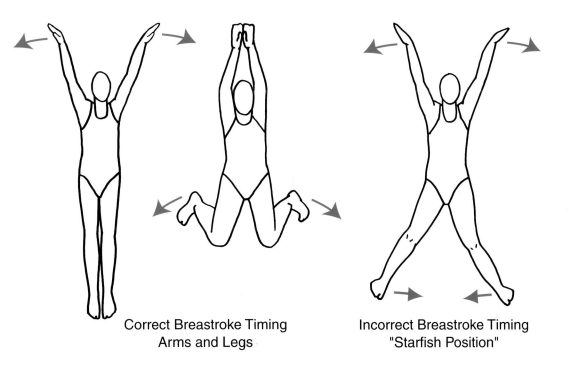

Correct Breastroke Timing
Arms and Legs

Incorrect Breastroke Timing
"Starfish Position"

Figure 3.32

Troubleshooting Breaststroke

My feet make a splash when I kick.

KICK It could be that your feet are not in a flexed position before you begin the power phase of your kick. If your toes are pointed, they will break the surface of the water and make a splash. If they are not flexed, you will also get minimal power from your kick.

BODY POSITION It could also be that you are swimming too flat. Remember, if your hips are not low when you draw your feet back to kick, there will not be enough water covering them. They will create a splash, and the effectiveness of your kick will be reduced as you kick air instead of water.

I don't move forward when I glide.

COORDINATION The most common cause of an ineffective glide is timing, specifically when the arm stroke and the kick are done simultaneously, not in succession: arms, then legs. When a swimmer has this incorrect timing, he or she appears like a starfish in the water, all limbs extended outward at the same time, making for the most unstreamlined body position possible. All potential forward motion for a glide is negated by the immense drag that results.

KICK It also might be that your kick is not producing enough power to give you glide momentum. Work on flexing your feet before you kick and holding your knees in a firm position, closer together than your feet. Kick in a rounded motion back to the center. You could also be drawing your knees up to your chest, rather than drawing your heels back to your hips. This makes a big difference in the amount of drag you produce and could be the difference between an productive or unproductive glide.

Breaststroke kick hurts my knees.

Breaststroke kick does put a great deal of torque on the knee joints. If you have a knee injury or condition and experience pain when doing the breaststroke kick, don't do it! Remember that pain is your warning system. Listen to it. Breaststroke is not supposed to hurt. If there is no underlying cause of your knee pain, it could be alleviated by changing your kicking technique. Make sure that your kick is rounded in its path, rather than angular. Kicking out, then squeezing the entire length of the leg together can be stressful to the knees. Also, be sure that your knees have some space between them when preparing to kick. Position them about shoulder width apart. Holding your knees too close together is hard on them. Conversely, positioning your knees, very far apart, so that your heels are closer together than your knees is equally stressful to the knee joints. Remember, it is the ankle that should do most of the rotation in the breaststroke kick.

KICK

I seem to stop dead in the water when I breathe.

Halted forward motion when breathing usually happens when the breathing is started too late in the arm stroke. If you begin breathing late, you have no lift from the natural leverage of the stroke. You are forced to press down with your arms in order to get your face out of the water to breathe. The result is that instead of moving forward, you just move up and down. Allow your face to come out of the water as your heels are drawing up toward your hips. You can also time your inhalation to occur as you turn the corner in your arm stroke, from outsweep to insweep.

COORDINATION

My arm stroke has no power.

In comparison to the kick, the arm stroke has very little power. But combined with the body motion, it is quite effective. Be sure you are not swimming flat, but utilizing a rocking motion that will give your arm stroke more leverage. Make sure that you are not pulling too deep. The outward sweep is done just under the surface, and inward sweep is no deeper than your chest. Try to think of the arm stroke as a sculling action, making sure that you hold onto the same water as you change the direction of the pull from outward to inward. Lastly, make sure that you are not breaking your lever by collapsing your elbows as you make your insweep. The elbows stay high and firm until the very end of the arm stroke when they fold in toward the ribs preparing for recovery.

BODY POSITION

ARM STROKE

5 Conditioning

5.1 THE PROCESS

Conditioning, often called "getting in shape," is the process of getting the body used to exercising. It involves subjecting the body to a workload it is not used to, then allowing the body to eventually adapt to that workload, resulting in the body becoming able to do more swimming faster. The process of conditioning involves the development of the cardiovascular and respiratory systems, the toning of existing muscle, and the building of new muscle. Through the process of conditioning, these systems work together to increase the body's capacity for endurance and speed (Figure 3.33).

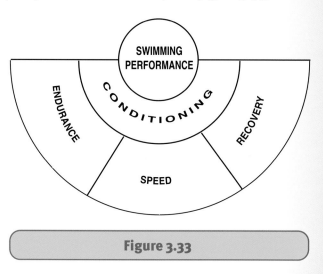

SWIMMING PERFORMANCE
CONDITIONING
ENDURANCE
RECOVERY
SPEED

Figure 3.33

Illustrated on a graph, the process of conditioning does not yield results in a steady upward trend. Instead, the results of conditioning take a path similar to a staircase (Figure 3.34). There are periods of obvious improvement, followed by periods known as plateaus, where all the work that a swimmer does seems to make no difference. To avoid getting discouraged during the process of conditioning, this real path of improvement is an important thing to remember.

There is no cut and dry timeline for conditioning to produce results. It is a very individual thing, with many variables, including level of fitness at the beginning of the process and the amount of time a swimmer needs to recover and adapt. A skilled coach will design a conditioning program with these issues in mind. For Masters swimmers, the main issue is recovery. Periods for recovery are as important in the process as periods of work. Without periods of recovery, adaptation to the workload will not happen well. In fact, as we age, longer periods of recovery are generally required. In most cases, Masters swimmers should not swim everyday.

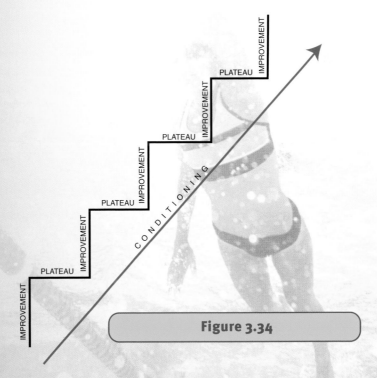

Figure 3.34

They should instead skip a day between workouts, or at least every third day, allowing time for their bodies to recover. If they don't allow recovery time, they will learn to swim tired, and the trend of improving endurance and speed will stop because adaptation will not really occur. Also significant is the issue of a swimmer's activity level at the beginning of the conditioning process. Some swimmers are able to start out doing 3,000 yards, while others can only do

1,000 yards. Good results from a conditioning program happen when the percentage of each individual swimmer's potential workload is increased incrementally, rather than when all swimmers start with the identical workload and increase the same amount. The improvement curve is not a function of how much a swimmer swims but is instead related more to what a swimmer is capable of doing. When a swimmer achieves adaptation to a certain level of workload, there are two ways to proceed in order to maintain the trend of improvement. First, a swimmer may swim the same amount of work but do it faster. Second, a swimmer's workload may be increased in time and quantity. A plan of combining these two approaches in an alternating pattern works well for many swimmers to produce more endurance and speed.

Finally, the process of conditioning is just that: a process. Keeping this in mind, swimmers should strive to experience the process fully, instead of just looking beyond it to the goal of "being in shape." The process of conditioning is, in fact, ongoing as a swimmer continues to reach for further improvement. It is a good feeling to improve. It is an equally good feeling to work toward improvement.

5.2 ELEMENTS OF A WORKOUT

When planning a workout, a good coach has a goal in mind for the swimmers doing the workout. Whether that goal is general conditioning, swim meet readiness, stroke versatility, or something else, the elements of the workout are not random. In addition, the specific combination of elements are designed to help swimmers reach the goal most effectively. This is why swimmers are encouraged to stay for the entire workout, even if they don't finish each set completely. It is like when your mother served you dinner as a child. There were several foods on the plate. Mom was really happy when you ate everything. And she wasn't happy at all when you ate all the chicken but didn't touch your peas and carrots. But, if you ate some of everything, Mom was usually okay with it because she knew you got the full range of nutrients. Getting the most out of a workout is the same way. If you get out halfway through, you miss some of the beneficial elements entirely. Sometimes it can't be avoided, but as a regular practice, staying for the whole workout gives you a more well-rounded fitness result.

In general, a swimming workout includes the following elements:

Warm up

The first activity of a workout is the warm-up, which allows swimmers to prepare their bodies to work by loosening up joints and muscles, increasing blood circulation, and practicing good stroke technique at a relaxed but sustained speed. The warm-up is best quantified in minutes, rather than yards. A good warm-up should consist of at least ten minutes of sustained swimming.

Kicking

Kicking early in the workout serves as a secondary warm-up. The large muscles in the legs carry a great deal of oxygen-rich blood through them. Kicking raises the heart rate a little, easing the swimmer's systems further into work mode. Of all the kicks, flutter kick, both on front and back, is the most aerobic, and the best choice for warm-up-type sets. Kicking may also be used to increase speed with short distance sets and to build endurance by kicking as a part of a long swim set. Lastly, kicking may be used as recovery, or "active rest," where there is no interval or goal time, just medium-strength kicking while the swimmer's heart rate has an opportunity to return to a lower rate, while he or she is still moving.

Pulling

Many coaches use pulling as stroke work. Truly, a pull buoy does correct the body position of most swimmers, giving them the feeling of how they are supposed to float without the pull buoy. Alternating pulling and swimming, by 200 or more, is a good exercise to bridge the improved body position that pulling gives to unassisted swimming. In addition to accentuating body position, pulling with a pull buoy should be used to focus on generating swimming power from the core.

Many swimmers report that pulling stresses their shoulders. This is because they are moving through the water flat, getting power from their shoulders, rather than rolling into each pull using their core. Once stroke technique is corrected, pulling can be used to build endurance with long distance pull sets. Sprint pulling is of little value because most swimmers find pulling easier than when they use their legs, too. Sprint pulling is also risky to vulnerable shoulders.

Pulling is widely accepted as a freestyle activity. There is disagreement about using a pull buoy with other strokes. In this coach's opinion, backstroke pulling is not very productive because with the arm stroke being out to the side of the body, the feet wag from side to side if they are not in motion, making pulling backstroke an exercise in correcting one's direction, rather than anything else. Using a pull buoy in butterfly commonly results in lower back pain due to the added pressure of raising and lowering the hips while the floatation device works to keep the hips stable. The same thing is true for breaststroke, although pulling breaststroke without a pull buoy, and using a light dolphin kick is an excellent complement, or alternative exercise to pulling freestyle with a pull buoy.

Stroke Drills

Including stroke drills in a workout allows swimmers the opportunity to focus on their technique. Basically, a stroke drill is an exercise that isolates a single aspect of a stroke in order to emphasize correct form. It is very important for swimmers to understand exactly what point is being emphasized by a particular stroke drill. If not, a swimmer may not focus on the right thing, or on nothing at all, as many stroke drills are awkward and may seem tedious at first. Some stroke drills are done at slow speed to emphasize proper float position, or stroke path. Other stroke drills are done at "swimming speed" to emphasize accessing power or identifying the correct muscle group to use. A very beneficial use of stroke drills is to alternate them with the regular stroke, allowing swimmers to first isolate a skill, then to immediately put it into practice by swimming the stroke.

Endurance Sets

Endurance sets bring to mind long distance swimming. A coach may have the swimmers swim a mile, or several 500s, to gauge progress. There is another kind of endurance set that is very useful to the general conditioning of swimmers and also improves pace skills, as well as swimmer confidence. It requires a pace clock to be on deck. Known as interval training, this kind of set calls for a number of repetitions of a short distance to be done, with each swim, along with a short rest period after each swim, to be completed within a specific time interval. For instance: the coach may ask for a set of "ten 100s on the 1:30." This means that swimmers have a minute and a half to swim 100 yards and to rest, before they are to do the same thing again, until they have done it ten times in a row. Usually, the rest period for an endurance interval set like this would be relatively short, giving the swimmer just enough recovery so he or she can complete the whole set.

One variation on interval training is "descending sets," in which swimmers are challenged to make each swim time faster than the previous swim, while staying on the same interval. Another variation is to increase the distance of each swim while keeping the rest the same. This sort of set is called a "ladder," or a "pyramid," if the set goes up in distances and then back down.

Interval training is a great way to gain the conditioning needed to swim a long distance faster, because while accomplishing the same overall distance as a straight long distance swim, the short rest periods taken with interval training allow the swimmer to recuperate just enough to swim faster than they would without that little rest. Through interval training, the body gets used to swimming faster for a long period of time.

I.M. Sets

Most swimmers have a favorite stroke, or maybe two. Many swimmers have a stroke that they can get by with, but it wouldn't be their first or second choice. And almost every swimmer has a stroke that is hard for them, that no matter how much they work on it, it is just never quite as easy for them as the other strokes. Still, many coaches believe that swimming versatility is important and have their swimmers practice all the strokes. I.M., or Individual Medley is a swim that encompasses all four competitive strokes, in the order of butterfly, backstroke, breaststroke and freestyle.

I.M. swimming has many benefits. First, by performing all the strokes, swimmers gain more well-rounded muscle development, as each stroke uses the major swimming muscles in a slightly different way. Swimmers who practice I.M. develop improved balance in the water. Because most swimmers have what they would characterize as a worst stroke, it is likely that stroke is not used a great deal by choice. If it weren't for I.M., some swimmers would avoid swimming their weak stroke completely. Swimmers who do practice their worst stroke do improve it, even if it may never become their favorite stroke!

Swimming I.M.s gives swimmers the opportunity to compare and contrast the way they swim the different strokes. They can ask themselves, "What is it that makes my freestyle work, while my backstroke is so hard?" This question can be a comparison of body position, breathing rhythm, stroke coordination, or kicking, among other things. Excellent "stroke contrasts" include: freestyle and backstroke, freestyle and butterfly, and breaststroke and butterfly. Even if swimmers are not going to do an I.M. in competition, I.M. swimming is a great way to add variety to a workout. For those who are competitive I.M.ers, swimming I.M.s is essential for practicing transitions, strategy and pace.

Sprint Sets

Sprinting is a favorite activity for many swimmers. It is quick, exciting, and fun. For adult swimmers, it is also extremely beneficial to practice sprinting, because as we age, our muscle fiber becomes less and less accustomed to doing explosive bursts of activity.

We must actively train our muscles to sprint, or muscles lose the ability to do it. Sprinting requires swimmers to swim as fast as they can. Sprints are usually very short swims of one or two lengths of the pool. Sprint sets can resemble interval training in some ways. Usually a number of repeats are done, with rest periods after each. However, it is important to keep in mind that true sprinting requires a good amount of rest. Without adequate rest, swimmers are not able to swim with speed, and the goal of the set cannot be achieved. Doing a number of sprints with only the same short rest as in endurance sets, does not train muscles to sprint, it trains for endurance.

Sprinting is used for meet preparation in a variety of ways. Some coaches have their swimmers do "broken swims," for instance. In a "broken swim," an athlete who is training for a 200 is asked to swim a 100, then a 50, then two 25s as fast as he can. After subtracting the rest periods, a race time can be theoretically estimated. Sprinting is also used to practice "race simulation," during the last phase of preparation for a big event. During this time, swimmers back off on the amount of training they do, and instead are asked to do more quality swimming in advance of their event. This kind of sprint set is not made up of many repetitions but can be only one swim of a particular event, at top speed.

Sprinting is a very demanding activity and can leave swimmers tired even one or two days afterwards. It is therefore recommended that sprint sets be spaced well over a training phase.

Cool Down

Cooling down is a much overlooked element of a workout. The importance of doing this should not be ignored. "Swimming down" allows the heart to return to its non-work mode and signals the body that recovery can begin. It provides a chance for the lactic acid produced during hard work to be rinsed from the muscles, avoiding potential soreness. Cool down also gives the swimmer the opportunity to reflect on his or her swimming, on what was great, and what could be done better next time. A good cool down should not be rushed and, like a warm-up, should not be a matter of yards, but a matter of time, lasting a minimum of ten minutes.

5.3 DRY LAND TRAINING

The benefits of dry land training are well known in terms of swimming performance and injury prevention. Dry land training is not a replacement for training in the water but is an excellent enhancement to a swimmer's training routine. Masters swimmers are encouraged to find time to build a dry land component into their training schedule. For adult athletes, dry land training is an extremely effective way to build and retain the capabilities of youthful muscles used for swimming.

The original theory of dry land training put forth in the early 1800s was that swimmers could improve their swimming technique by practicing on the land with the assistance of various apparatuses designed to simulate the movements of swimming. Researchers soon realized that swimming was more than mechanical motion and that training in the water was essential in experiencing a feel for the water and developing a streamlined path through the water. By the early 20th century, dry land training again became the subject of study, but this time for the purpose of athletic performance in swimming. Researchers observed that swimmers who participated in specific dry land training improved quicker than those who just trained in the water. It became clear that the role of dry land training for swimmers was to accelerate the rate of muscle development, which could be applied to swimming.

Aspects of Swimming Enhanced by Dry Land Training

Of the many factors that influence swimming performance, conditioning is one that is most directly enhanced by dry land training (Figure 3.35). As previously discussed, swimming conditioning is the process of training the muscles to adapt to work, leading to improvement in endurance and speed. Both of these things can be very well learned in the water but it is quicker on land. Perhaps even more important though, dry land training is especially effective in maintaining and increasing the flexibility needed for optimum swimming performance. Without flexibility, the benefits of improved strength and endurance cannot be fully utilized. Among adult athletes, flexibility is usually the hardest physical skill to maintain, as it naturally decreases with age. Studies have shown that regular practice of quality flexibility exercises can slow this process. Good flexibility improves body position, range of motion, and the ability to access strength and power. It is therefore directly connected to correct swimming technique. Masters swimmers who include a program of flexibility work into their training are taking a proactive step in reducing the risk of injury associated with technique problems, in addition to improving their conditioning.

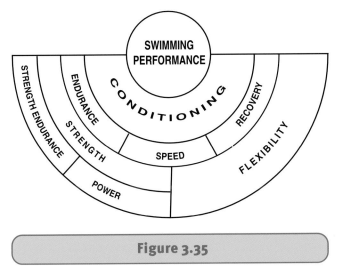

Figure 3.35

FLEXIBILITY

Flexibility exercise, commonly called stretching, is a very beneficial activity when done correctly. However, experts agree that stretching should be done after the muscles are warmed up or it can, ironically, result in injury. Also, careful attention should be paid to stretching technique and body alignment. Optimally, stretching should be part of every workout. Some experts believe that stretching is best done before swimming, in order to prepare the body for the workout. Some experts believe that it is most beneficial after swimming, when the body is most warmed up. Some experts believe that stretching both before and after workout produces the best flexibility results. If done before swimming, a few minutes of jogging, skipping rope or bike riding are good ways to warm up before initiating a stretching routine.

The act of stretching requires patience and must not be rushed. Forcing a muscle to stretch quickly beyond its range can be worse than not stretching at all. Short jerky movements actually make the muscles contract in a protective reflex, defeating the whole purpose of stretching, which is to elongate the muscles for better flexibility. Stretching is a gradual process that yields results over time. Every stretch should be slow and smooth, bringing the stretch to its maximum range, and holding it there for a minimum of five to ten seconds before releasing it slowly to a relaxed state. Knowing your own maximum range in any particular stretching exercise is important and must be determined by you. Listen to your body.

Stretching should not hurt. Don't be pressured by trying to stretch to the same degree as another athlete. Everyone is different. Stretching becomes easier as range of motion improves over time. Finally, executing each stretch with good posture and proper support is important in order to get the specific benefit that a particular stretching exercise is designed to produce. An experienced coach or trainer can help with this. Photos A-N show stretches to improve flexibility for swimmers.

With hands behind head, pull head forward stretching neck muscles

Pull head to side, while pressing opposite arm downward, stretching side of neck

Pull left to right, stretching triceps and shoulder

With left hand behind shoulder blades, pull left elbow to right, stretching lats

With forearm braced at right angle, twist chest away from fixed position, stretching chest

Bend to 90 degrees at waist and press chest down, stretching back

In sitting position, with soles of feet together, pull soles of feet toward you and allow knees to fall apart, stretching legs

Balancing on right leg in a squatting position, extend left leg to side, stretching inner leg

Lying on back, draw knees to chest, pressing spine firmly into the floor, stretching hamstrings and back

Lying on back with right leg extended, draw left knee to chest, stretching leg

Lying on back with right leg extended, lift left leg to 90 degrees as straight as possible, stretching leg

In standing position, balance on left leg and pull right foot toward buttocks, stretching quads

In standing position with legs shoulder width apart, bend upper body to side, stretching torso

In sitting position with legs extended, cross right leg over left leg, holding it with left arm, and turn torso to right

STRENGTH AND POWER

Strength is an essential ingredient in any athlete's ability to perform and avoid injury. There are three kinds of strength that can be developed: maximum strength, strength endurance, and power. Only the latter two correspond to swimming performance. Maximum strength, or the ability to lift as much weight as possible, is not as important in swimming as it is in many other sports.

However, strength endurance and power are specifically linked to swimming well. Strength endurance is important in a swimmer being able to maintain the use of strength over time without tiring. Power refers to the swimmer's ability to apply strength to produce speed. Although swimming requires both of these types of strength, distance swimming uses more strength endurance, while sprinting uses more power.

Many experts believe that strength training should be done close in time to a swimming workout in order to maximize the transfer effects. Others believe that strength training and swimming should be done on alternating days to avoid fatigue and allow time for recovery, especially for older adults. Dry land training for strength development of swimmers is best pursued through a blend of general weight bearing exercises that develop the arms, legs and trunk and resistance exercises that simulate swimming, using the muscle groups in combination.

In a gym, free weights and some weight machines are good for developing general strength of specific muscle groups (Figure 3.36). Activities that duplicate the path of the pull and the leverage used in swimming are found on pulley-type machines or equipment with adjustable hydraulic resistance. It is important to remember that when using weights and weight machines to benefit swimming performance, lifting the heaviest weights possible is not very helpful. When lifting weights, the weight should be controlled up and down. The most effective way to use weights to build strength that is applicable to swimming is to use only enough weight so that many repetitions of an exercise can be done in a row, simulating the repetitive actions of swimming. To train for strength endurance, more repetitions are done at a rate resembling the swimmer's stroke rate. Weight should amount to more than the resistance of the water but

Bench Press

Pull Over

Rowing

Curl

Heel Raises

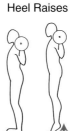

Squat

Clean & Jerk

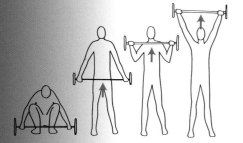

French Curl

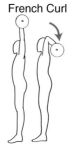

Back Press

Foward Butterflies

Reverse Butterflies

Tricep Lift

Standing Butterflies

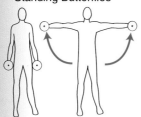

Horizontal Rowing

Figure 3.36   Strength Training with Weights

not so much that the full range of the motion of the exercise is compromised. Commonly, five to ten sets of up to 25 repetitions of a single exercise are appropriate. To direct the exercise to increase power, the number of repetitions should decrease to 3 to 5 sets of 6 to 10 repetitions, with a slightly increased weight. Weight training exercises can also be measured by time, with more time spent doing strength endurance sets and less time for power work.

Probably the most effective and least expensive way to get swimming-specific strength training is with a stretch band made of surgical tubing or bungie-type cord. A stretch band allows the swimmer to very closely duplicate the motions of swimming and to easily adjust resistance. It is light and fits into any swim bag. Stretch band work can be done at home, at the pool, or at the gym. Excellent stretch band exercises are illustrated in photos O – T.

O-Q Simultaneous Stroke Simulation: With arms extended at the same height as the stretch band, hold upper body firm and pull arms back, keeping elbows high, maintaining speed to the end of the movement

Alternating Arm Simulation: Same as O-Q, only one arm at a time

131

S-T Butterfly:

Standing with back toward stretch band, with arms extended in back at shoulder level, pull hands to front at shoulder level

A stretch band is also one of the most effective tools in doing specific exercises to strengthen, stablize and rehabilitate the shoulder (Figure 3.37). Two other exercises complete this extremely important shoulder set. These two exercises can be done with a soup can or other light weight household object. If time is limited for strength training, these four exercises targeting the four muscles of the rotator cuff should be prioritized. Like flexibility training, strength training should be done after a full-body warm-up. Proper body position and technique are essential in reaping the benefits of this activity. A coach or trainer should assist with this and should be present with any use of free weights. Stretching is advised after a strength training workout.

1. OUTWARD ROTATION

Using a stretch band
- Keep elbow tight to side
- Keep hand at a right angle to shoulder
- Keep wrist firm at neutral
- Swing forearm outward like a door – not past midline

2. INWARD ROTATION

Using a stretch band
- Keep elbow tight to side
- Keep hand at a right angle to shoulder
- Keep wrist firm at neutral
- Swing forearm inward like a door – not past midline

3. VERTICAL LIFT

Using a soup can
- Hold can like it is a cup of water
- Keep wrist firm at neutral
- Lift can straight up the middle until hand, wrist and shoulder are parallel

4. DIAGONAL LIFT

Using a soup can
- Hold can with thumb down
- Keep wrist firm at neutral
- Lift can with straight arm at 45 degrees from front no farther than halfway to shoulder height

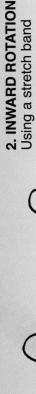
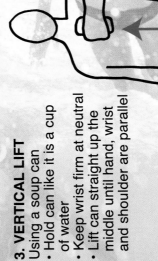

Figure 3.37 Shoulder Stability Exercises

ENDURANCE

A swimmer's general endurance and cardiovascular capabilities are most successfully trained in the water. Accomplished athletes with extreme endurance on land find themselves unable to sustain swimming for a substantial length of time or to recover from swimming activities quickly without devoting time to training in the water.

However, swimmers who add land exercise for endurance into their training routine find that they are more able to do more swimming without fatigue. For adult athletes especially, endurance training on land seems to benefit swimming endurance prominently, enabling Masters swimmers to do longer workouts and faster distance swimming.

The following activities are recommended to enhance swimming endurance:

1. Jogging or running
2. Hiking
3. Biking
4. Cross country skiing
5. Kayaking, canoeing, rowing
6. Water aerobics

These activities should be done steadily at an intensity that is sustainable 20 to 60 minutes.

Dry land training is an extremely beneficial activity to add to any swimming routine. It enhances conditioning done in the water in many ways. Even if increased speed and endurance are not your goals, dry land training is especially important to Masters swimmers to improve flexibility and prevent injuries.

6 Achieving Better Swimming

Of the many factors that affect swimming performance (Figure 3.38), one cannot be isolated as the most important. They are connected, and one aspect affects another. Achieving better swimming is a matter of developing a well-balanced workout routine that encompasses swimming technique work, conditioning in the water, and dry land training.

By doing so, you develop your ability to eliminate drag, feel the water and access potential power, while developing your endurance, speed and the ability to recover, along with increasing your flexibility, strength and power. When you work to achieve better swimming, you are working toward more efficient and more sustainable swimming, which is just more enjoyable.

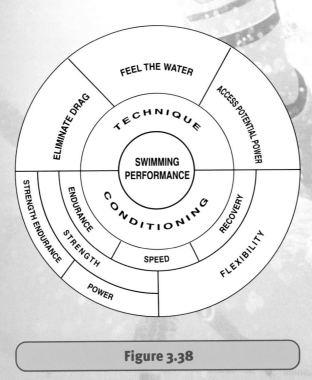

Figure 3.38

CHAPTER 4
THE MASTERS
SWIM TEAM

Swimming is both a team and individual sport. To experience it fully, a swimmer must belong to a team. Masters swimming has been built through the swim team experience. Masters swimmers thrive in the team environment, where they swim side by side, each reaching for a unique goal, where camaraderie surrounds them, and where adult swimming fitness is the common denominator.

1 Finding an Existing Team

1.1 WHERE TO LOOK

More and more, Masters swim teams are becoming part of the regular programming offered at many swim centers. Chances are you will be able to find an existing team within a short drive of your home or your work. Start by locating the swimming pools in your area, and then make a few phone calls, or do a little web surfing to determine which pools in your area offer Masters swimming programs. A good starting place is to look for pools offering Masters swimming through city recreation departments, public school districts, colleges and universities, and YMCAs. You may also be able to get some good leads by asking other adult athletes.

1.2 WHAT YOU WANT

When looking for a team to join, you should think about what is important to you in a swimming program. For instance, you might be particularly interested in swimming in an outdoor pool. It might be a priority for you to swim with people of your same age. You might be looking for a coach specializing in distance swimming. You might be looking for a team with an easy-going attitude. These are some of the considerations that are really a matter of personal preference. Finding a team that "fits" your needs and expectations is important in developing a long lasting, beneficial and enjoyable relationship with Masters swimming.

WHAT TO ASK

1.3

When making contact with a team representative, you might want to have a series of questions ready to help you learn more about the team. These questions may include:

- What is the workout schedule?
- What is the cost?
- How would a swimmer of your level fit in?
- About how many swimmers attend each workout?
- Does the team compete?
- How many yards are done at an average workout?
- How much time is devoted to technique?

Some Masters swim teams have a policy that new swimmers must try out for a few workouts before officially joining. Beyond asking questions, actually participating in the team's activities is probably the best way to determine if there is a good "fit," and whether your expectations of a swimming program will be met.

2 Structuring a New Team

If there isn't a Masters swim team operating in your area, you could start one. It is a very exciting proposition to set up a new team. If you are up to the challenge, there are many factors that must be examined in order to create a team structure that will operate smoothly and continue over the long term.

As with most endeavors, research and planning is essential to success. Working out details in advance is the best way to ensure a strong program, that will not collapse when obstacles arise. Some things that should be defined before your team begins are:

2.1 PHILOSOPHY

Defining a new team's approach to swimming and direction is important in establishing a foundation on which to build. Many teams develop a Mission Statement, which states their philosophy. The Mission Statement is a concise expression of the team's philosophy, which usually outlines:

- who the team will serve
- the general focus of the team
- the benefits that will occur from the team

The following are two examples of Mission Statements:

Mission Statement of the Richmond Sharks

The Richmond Sharks will exist to provide the community with a dynamic, coach-driven competitive swim program that will promote a life-long love of swimming and benefit the whole person by focusing on:

- Swimming excellence through ongoing technique and conditioning work
- A positive and supportive environment that emphasizes good sportsmanship, team work, positive self image and work ethic
- Ongoing opportunities for healthy competition

Mission Statement of the West Bend Otters

The mission of the West Bend Otters is to make the pursuit of better swimming available to adult athletes by providing high level coaching, challenging workouts and competition for team members.

THE BUSINESS OF THE TEAM

2.2

Planning how team business will be handled is essential in setting up a smoothly operating Masters swimming program. There are three ways in which the business operations of swim teams are commonly structured. The first is when the swim team is a program sponsored or run entirely by a city, school district or other larger entity.

In this case, the operations are handled by that larger entity. The finances, employees, and schedule are all taken care of by that entity. There are many reasons that teams seek this sort of structure. First and foremost, there is no financial risk for the team. With all expenses covered, including pool time, coach's salary and equipment, more attention can be paid to the swimming activities of the program.

On the other hand, there are drawbacks. A team can be under constant pressure to prove its value or risk losing its pool time. Also, many times, the team has no input in who makes up the coaching staff. Sometimes the coach may be simply a lifeguard assigned to the task. The team may also not get the support it needs because important decisions are made by managers who are not necessarily interested in Masters swimming. While very safe in terms of financial responsibility, this kind of team structure gives very little control to the team.

The second way a team may structure its operations is as a non-profit organization, with a board of directors, usually made up of team members, which makes the business and operational decisions for the team. This is a popular way to organize a team because it gives the team complete control over its own operations and direction. The team chooses its own coaching staff. The team makes its own rules and procedures. Everyone involved is dedicated to swimming.

The major drawback of this model is that the organization is usually run by volunteers, who may or may not have the time needed to devote to team operations. At times, the work may fall unevenly to a few individuals, or to one person, which can lead to resentment. Important business can be left undone. Also, as a non-profit organization, the team needs to bring in enough money to pay for its own pool time, coach and equipment, through team dues. If dues do not equal expenses, the organization must cut back its hours and employees, or devote its time and energy to fundraising campaigns. The benefits of this kind of structure are very positive, but it is labor intensive to make it work right over the long term.

To curb expenses, some teams running as non-profit organizations use a rotating coach method. On these teams, each team member volunteers to coach the other members of the team for a day or a week at a time. Everyone takes a turn, and the expense of a paid coach is eliminated. This sort of cost-saving measure depends on the cooperation of every swimmer. It usually yields some very creative workouts but makes continuity of conditioning and technique an issue of concern.

The third kind of structure is a coach run program. In this case, the coach operates the business of the team, as well as doing the coaching. He or she collects dues, pays for the pool rental, and he or she gets what is left over as compensation. The strengths of this kind of structure include a coach who is probably highly motivated to run an excellent program.

A coach who "owns" a team will usually have a clear vision of what a great swim team should be and be highly dedicated to its success. Growth of the team and athlete development will probably be top priorities. On the down side, running a team is a huge job that takes ongoing attention, leading to the possible burnout of the coach if he or she is not getting the compensation worthy of the job. For a small team, adequate compensation for the coach could mean more expensive swimming for team members. Many coach-run programs are very successful. Others are short lived.

COACHING

On any successful sports team, the coach is recognized as an important force in the team's morale, development and success. The coach is usually seen as the leader of the team, someone who possesses experience and knowledge of the sport, the ability to teach, challenge and motivate athletes, and the presence to unify, mobilize and drive the team to new heights. The most successful Masters swim teams have coaches who fit this description.

When selecting a swim coach for your new team, it is important to remember that the coach will be seen as the face of your team. The coach that you choose will be a major factor in attracting new swimmers and retaining the swimmers on your team. When looking at candidates, considering those with experience in competitive swimming may or may not be a good choice. Although such a candidate will have an understanding of the swim team environment, being a good swimmer does not necessarily mean a person is a good coach. A candidate with experience coaching swimming brings an understanding of the requirements of leadership, time management, and workout structure. Direct experience with adult athletes is even better, as there are distinct differences in coaching youth and Masters swimming. Experience in teaching swimming is also a desirable quality as many adults join Masters swimming with only basic swimming skills. A candidate with experience teaching advanced swimming technique is highly desirable, as improving swimming efficiency is an ongoing quest of Masters swimmers.

Coaching Masters Swimmers

Coaching Masters swimmers is a very rewarding experience. A coach shares the excitement of an adult swimmer who learns a new skill, the pride of an adult swimmer who exceeds his or her own expectations, and the exhilaration of an adult athlete who continues to defy age. These feelings shared by coach and athlete are genuine and remarkable.

The relationship that develops between an athlete and coach is quite special. Unlike the relationship of a youth athlete and an adult coach, which is at its base unequal in terms of power, knowledge, and life experience, the relationship of a Masters swimmer and his or her coach is in many ways that of equals. It can be seen as a partnership between two adults, who each have something to bring to the experience. When both athlete and coach are involved in decisions, a different dynamic is present. The athlete may choose to focus on butterfly technique, and the coach will come up with drills to improve the swimmer's stroke. The coach will lay out a training program for a particular swim meet, and the athlete will make the decision on what events to train for.

With swimming at the center, at times the swimmer can take the lead and at other times the coach can take the lead. This kind of partnership is based in mutual respect and trust. It is a working relationship, which  is as close as many friendships. Coaching Masters swimming is also very challenging. The partnership between Masters athlete and coach is sometimes tested. For instance, a Masters swimmer may decide not to do what the coach has assigned, not because of a health limitation, but just because he or she doesn't want to. When an adult athlete chooses not to do something, the coach has no real authority to make him or her do it.

The coach cannot send the swimmer home with a note to his or her parent, or order him or her to swim a 500 butterfly for disobedience. Instead, the coach must be flexible and creative in maintaining the partnership. Without compromising the team's activities, the coach may offer an alternate activity that accomplishes the same goal as the set that was rejected. If a particular swimmer frequently decides to do their own thing, a private conversation may be called for, in order to reestablish the coach/athlete partnership. The swimmer's goals should be discussed, and it should be determined how they can be met in the Masters swimming group workout environment.

Some Masters swimmers are also reluctant to try new things presented by the coach. They may spend an undue amount of time and energy analyzing a newly presented technique and justifying why the old way is good enough, leaving little or no opportunity to actually try it. Although swimming is considered a "thinking sport," some Masters swimmers can get bogged down in trying to understand new things intellectually and rationalizing why not to try them. This can lead to long discussions with the coach in the middle of a workout. A coach cannot force a reluctant swimmer to swim a new way. A coach can only offer the new skill as an opportunity for a new experience. Reluctant swimmers should be encouraged to have fun with new experiences. With a supportive, non-judgemental partnership, trying a new skill can be less threatening. New horizons can become things to approach together.

Coaching a Masters Swim Team

While the diversity of Masters swimmers is one of its highlights, it also presents one of the biggest challenges to creating a sense of a team. Team dynamics are different in Masters swimming than in youth swimming. On youth competitive swim teams, the common goal of all swimmers is to compete as a team. In Masters swimming, this is not a goal shared by everyone.

Some Masters swimmers compete but others swim for fitness. Still others swim purely for the social opportunities. There is also the matter of the wide range of swimming ability and ages in Masters swimming. The needs of a national class swimmer are different than a novice swimmer. And the needs of an 85-year-old swimmer are different than those of a 25-year-old swimmer. With so many different agendas, and so many levels of ability, a coach has a big job in meeting the various needs of the swimmers on the team and keeping them all "swimming" in the same direction. The unifying factor of

Masters swimming that must kept in mind is adult swimming fitness. This is what all of these swimmers have in common. The task of the coach is to emphasize this commonality, despite the distinct differences among individuals and unify the team's activities toward this goal. This is sometimes easier said than done. At times, the needs of a national class sprinter will seem to be at odds with the needs of a distance swimmer. An 85-year-old swimmer may not be served well by doing the same set as a younger fitness swimmer. With all of these swimmers in the pool at the same time, how can a coach meet each individual's needs, while successfully creating a sense of team and unified team workouts? Here are some ideas:

1. Create "distance lanes" and "sprint lanes" for a main set, with each set requiring about the same length of time.

2. Have faster swimmers do more repetitions of a set and slower swimmers do fewer, so they finish at approximately the same time.

3. Build options into sets.

4. Assign swims by time instead of distance. For instance, have everyone do a 10-minute swim.

5. Assign "social kicking" to all swimmers at the same time.

All of these ideas require excellent time management, set editing, and awareness of each individual's needs by the coach.

It may seem, at times, that a coach is running six workouts at once. Done well, this kind of individualized workout will have a very unified feeling as swimmers finish sets together, rest together, do heads-up activities, such as kicking together, and complete the workout and cool down together.

Another job of a team coach is to make sure every swimmer knows that his or her participation on the team is important. The essence of successful team is that each individual is a valued part of the group. Accomplishing this requires the coach to connect personally with every swimmer, and to maintain that connection. A good coach should have direct interaction with every single swimmer in the pool during a workout. The dialogue with each swimmer will be different.

With one, a coach may discuss backstroke technique. With another, the coach will talk about an upcoming swim meet. With another swimmer, there will be congratulations on a promotion. And with another, a troublesome shoulder might be addressed. With still another, the recent death of a parent can be touched upon. And yet another, a coach may suggest moving up a lane. Another swimmer will announce to the coach that she is pregnant. Some conversations focus on swimming directly, some focus more on  the swimmer, and seem to have nothing to do with swimming. The pool becomes a place where each swimmer feels connected to the team through swimming, as well as through the coach.

Clearly, the job of coaching a Masters swim team is not an easy one! It takes an organized, caring, responsive, adaptable, knowledgeable, energetic and creative individual to bring a Masters swim team together. It is a very rewarding occupation.

WATER TIME

2.4

In order to have a successful Masters swim team, you must secure water time, so you can hold workouts. It is best to have a regular, predictable schedule in order to build continuity on the team. However, this is sometimes quite a challenge. Although Masters swimming is gaining popularity, it is sometimes difficult to get desirable water time. Often, Masters teams are given the leftovers: 5:00 a.m., 8:30 p.m., or even only on weekends, while other programs, including more valued youth swim teams, are given more and "better" hours. If you are lucky enough to get good water time, run with it! Make the most of it! But in the more common situation that you are presented with a poor schedule, you must be creative.

You might advertise an ungodly early morning time slot as a "Commuter Special." You might spin a non-ideal night workout as an "Unwinding Swim." Teams that are given only weekend pool time might have to become "dual pool teams" and pick up additional weekday hours at other pools to build a solid program. Over time, as your team grows in size, strength and popularity, you may find that you will be given better hours.

2.5 PROGRAM

A dynamic Masters Swimming program begins with a schedule of workouts but goes far beyond. It consists of mechanisms designed to draw new swimmers in, and keep them inspired to come back, allowing the program to grow and thrive. The program you set up is the way you "deliver" on your mission statement.

Continuity and Variety

The activities of your program should be exciting and interesting to swimmers, but they should also offer a sense of routine. Swimmers should know what to expect from your program in terms of the quality of the program and the coaching. When swimmers arrive for a workout, and it is cancelled either due to a time change or the coach not showing up, swimmers get discouraged quickly. Swimmers should know what to expect from the workout organization and atmosphere. Swimmers should always be greeted and welcomed by the coach on the pool deck. They should know what lane to go to and what to do when they first get in the water. Swimmers should also know what the expectations are in terms of actual swimming. They should know that they will get feedback on their strokes. They should know about how many yards the workouts are on average. They should know they will be challenged.

Continuity is important, but variety is important, too. The content and focus of workouts themselves should not be the same all the time or swimmers can get bored. Coaches who are creative in designing workouts give their swimmers a sense of curiosity and anticipation, and a reason to come back for another workout.

Feeder Programs

One way to create a steady flow of people into your program is through feeder programs. A feeder program is a developmental program, in which the next logical step is your swim team. Feeder programs that work well for Masters swim teams include:

SWIMMING LESSONS

Swimming lessons for adults are not offered enough. With good advertising, adult lesson programs are often well attended by adults of all ages. Many adults are actually embarrassed that they do not know how to swim and jump at the chance to learn swimming skills. Some beginning adult swimmers have had drowning and water anxiety issues since childhood and are very motivated to move beyond their fears. Many individuals just learning to swim will exhibit raw swimming talent, improve quickly, and they become confident, efficient swimmers. Adults feeling the success of their new swimming skills should be invited to join your swim team and continue to build their skills and enjoyment of swimming.

STROKE CLINICS

Stroke clinics work as feeder programs when people from the larger pool community are offered the opportunity to study and practice a swimming stroke as a one-time experience with a swimming expert, such as your Masters swim team coach.

A stroke clinic can be structured in many ways, but to be most meaningful to people not yet involved in Masters swimming, it should include a step-by-step explanation of the technique of the stroke being studied, a demonstration of that stroke, practice time and feedback. Using a blend of classroom activities, such as lecture and video, and water activities including stroke drills and guided practice, swimmers who attend a stroke clinic learn new and exciting things about their swimming. A stroke clinic, or series of clinics, put on by your team is a great way to introduce swimmers to what Masters swimming is all about.

Specialized Workouts

Offering specialized workouts gives swimmers an extra incentive to pursue a special swimming avenue in more detail. Specialized workouts should be offered in addition to regular team workouts, not instead of them, to avoid dividing the team. Specialized workouts tailored to certain groups and activities may change with the make up of your team. Specialized workouts can be held for:

SENIORS

Although many elderly swimmers participate fully in regular Masters swimming workouts, some express that they feel intimidated and often overlooked. Some seniors report that they feel pushed to the outside lanes, far from the main energy of the workout where younger swimmers swim faster and farther. A specialized workout for seniors, held once or twice a week is often very much appreciated. It is a time when they can set the pace, swim in the fast lane, and be the main focus of the workout.

OPEN WATER

Because open water swimming is one of the favorite Masters swimming activities, swimmers are often very interested in getting extra experience by training in an open water setting. Some teams meet once a week at a local lake or marina to swim together. Team open water swims are often very popular specialized workouts and attract new swimmers regularly. Special care should be taken to prepare new swimmers for their first open water experience.

Their swimming should be strong in both technique and endurance. They should be able to deal with colder temperatures than the pool, which are sometimes shocking to the body. They should be able to negotiate waves and currents, which can be deceptively strong and unnerving. It is a good practice to assign a buddy to a first-time open water swimmer, to ensure the experience is both pleasant and safe. The coach accompanying the group should be a certified lifeguard.

NATIONALS

Swimmers who set their sights on competing at a National Championship, or other high level swim meet will benefit from specialized workouts dedicated to their goal. A ten to twelve week program where your National team trains together twice a week, and with the whole team the rest of the time, will create strong morale and more specific conditioning results for your Nationals bound athletes. Training for high-level meets can be extremely demanding and stressful, and a dedicated workout time provides the opportunity for coach and athlete to devote direct attention toward a successful outcome to this effort of major proportions.

Special Team Activities

Special team activities are instrumental in developing a positive team atmosphere. Special events give swimmers something to look forward to as a team and create good memories for and about the team. These activities may include:

HOLIDAY WORKOUTS

Holidays offer an excellent opportunity to hold workouts because most people have the day off and enjoy spending some of their down time swimming. Holiday workouts are often the best attended workouts of the year. Many teams make holiday workouts into special occasions by offering extra challenging or themed workouts. Sometimes a brunch follows the workout.

Some teams "ring in the new year" with a memorable New Year's morning workout of extreme proportions! Some teams hold annual "Fitness Before the Feast" workouts early Thanksgiving morning. Some teams even celebrate the coach's birthday in holiday style by swimming 100 yards for each year of the coach's age. Holiday workouts offer teams the opportunity to establish and carry on tradition. They are talked about long after the holiday is over.

SOCIALS

Holding team social events effectively promotes a cohesive team. The social aspects of Masters swimming are as important to many swimmers as the swimming. A team gathering outside of the water deepens the bonds that swimmers have formed while swimming and makes the team further connected to the rest of their lives.

Social events may take many forms. Some teams have a monthly dinner at a favorite restaurant after one workout. Others have a potluck dinner, meeting at the home of a different team member each time. Some teams hold annual picnics, softball games or bike rides. Other Masters swimming favorites include:

Awards Banquet

An annual awards dinner is very meaningful to swimmers, as much for the recognition as it is for the team spirit. Swimmers and their families and guests should be invited to attend, making for a very large group to share the team's celebration.

Such an event can be successfully held in a restaurant banquet room, community center, or school auditorium. An awards banquet is an opportunity to honor the most outstanding swimmers on the team, from the very fastest, to the most improved, to the most inspirational, to the swimmer with the most team spirit. Some teams choose the recipients of these awards through a write-in ballot by team members. Some teams give this job to the coach. Being honored in this way is an extremely special event for an adult athlete.

Some teams create an award for every swimmer on the team, underscoring the importance of every swimmer's participation and effort. This is also the time to honor long-time team members by giving "5 Year" and "10 Year" awards. Awards for those who have volunteered their time in team service are also appropriate.

The opportunities for creative awards are endless. Inviting ideas for special awards from the team for particular swimmers often brings a very enthusiastic response. Awards can be given for:

- Most, or least, hair in a swim cap
- Best lane partner
- Most likely to swim 200 butterfly
- Best lap counting
- Fastest kicking without fins

A successful awards banquet can be an event that is anticipated throughout the year and can become a favorite tradition of the team.

Talent Show

This kind of event is designed to encourage swimmers to share more than swimming with their team mates. It is a very entertaining event and fascinating to see the array of talents, hobbies and interests among the swimmers of the team.

Many Swimmers play a variety of musical instruments. They sing and dance. They show their collections, their artwork, and their prized pets. They demonstrate cake decorating, orchid cultivation and crocheting. As swimmers share their "other talent" with the team, they share a special part of themselves, which is appreciated and supported by the team as much as the swimming that they already share.

Community Service Day

Some teams choose to make community service a team activity. Reaching out to the community as a team is great for the community and great for the team. A group of volunteers can accomplish a great deal together. A team experiences making a difference together. It is a very bonding activity. Litter clean up, helping out at a soup kitchen, planting trees in a community park, painting and doing repairs at a school are examples of projects that need volunteers. They are all ways that a team can give back to their community and do so together.

2.6 TEAM IDENTIFICATION

Nothing brings out the sense of team like a team uniform. As in all team sports, athletes wear their uniform proudly both at practice and in competition. A team in uniform creates a group identity that is clear to its own members and to other teams. Team uniforms are an important way to build team spirit. In Masters swimming, this uniform may be as simple as a team swim cap.

Some teams choose to have a more extensive uniform including team swimsuit, t-shirt, parka and towel. A team banner is also an important piece of team identification that promotes a sense of team. When it is hung up at the home pool, a team banner in effect, marks territory. When it is hung up at a swim meet, it is like a flag that identifies your team as a distinctive entity among others. A team banner is a symbol of a unity. Team wear and other team items can be imprinted with the name of the team or its abbreviation. Many teams choose team colors. Some teams develop logos and mascots to identify themselves.

TEAM COMMUNICATION

2.7

Team communication is important to keep everyone on the team informed and connected on matters including workout schedules, special events, competitions, meetings and team news. Because most Masters swimmers do not attend workouts everyday, announcements made at workouts have limited effectiveness. To make sure everyone knows what is going on with the team, additional methods of communication should be used. Some effective ways to communicate with the team include:

E-mail

E-mail has become a popular way for Masters swim teams to communicate. A regular weekly e-mail is a great way to keep most members of the team updated. This may take the form of a letter from the coach, or a simple list of announcements. Electronic communication is a great way to stay in touch with most team members but should be regularly updated. It should also be kept in mind that not everyone has e-mail.

Team Newsletter

Many teams publish traditional newsletters. A newsletter communicates important information, but even further, it is a way to promote team spirit and Master's swimming pride. Articles on the various swimming successes of team members, as well as stories of interest about adult athletics and the larger Masters swimming community are interesting to swimmers. Articles on stroke technique and conditioning principles are also read eagerly. Some teams use their newsletter to announce the "Swimmer of the Month." Photos and graphic elements give a newsletter even more appeal. Masters swimmers who do not have access to e-mail will still be informed if your team puts out a newsletter regularly. Even swimmers with e-mail will want to have a copy of the team newsletter. Many will be saved in scrapbooks and sent to relatives and friends.

Bulletin Board

Maintaining an attractive bulletin board at the team's home pool is a good way to get information to team members. It is a permanent and convenient place for team members to get information. The team bulletin board should be updated regularly with new content to be effective. If it is an outdoor bulletin board, weathered paper should be replaced frequently, or current information can appear like "old news."

Phone Tree

Some teams also use phone trees to pass on information. A phone tree works when one team member calls three other team members, who each call three more team members, and so on. This method is great for making personal contact, which is appreciated by many people. It also gets the team involved. Sometimes, the process does not work as designed when people are too busy to do their part.

MARKETING

2.8

Effective publicity is very important for a new team, as well as for an existing team. Getting the word out about your activities puts your Masters swimming program "on the map," enabling new people to find you. Successful marketing must be directed to those who might be interested in what you are doing. This requires you to know your "market," and to target that audience with your efforts. At its most basic, the target audience of Masters swimming is the adult population. More specifically, it can include:

- Lap swimmers and those wishing to improve their swimming
- Triathletes and other athletes looking to cross-train
- Ex-competitive swimmers of all ages
- Those looking for a new fitness routine
- Those looking for camaraderie
- Those who enjoy a team environment

The market for potential new swimmers is quite expansive! This gives you the opportunity to be creative in your marketing. It is usually most effective to use a variety of marketing methods at once, to connect with the most people. Good marketing methods include:

Web site

Many teams maintain a Web site with general information on practice times and locations. Some teams also include a history of the team, a bio of the coach, team records, and other distinctive features about their team. Making sure your team's Web site has wide search parameters is important. Key words beyond Masters swimming and adult fitness will expand the potential audience of your Web site. Some good key terms include: novice swimmers, senior fitness, swimming technique, over 18 swim team, competition and coached workout. There are many others.

Printed Material

Some teams distribute brochures and flyers with workout schedules in public places that are frequented by people in their target audience. Good locations include community centers, gyms, sports stores, cafés and senior centers. It is sometimes necessary to get permission to distribute, post or leave a stack of material in certain locations. The brochure or printed piece that you distribute works as the first impression of your team. Make it good! It should be attractive and concise. People who see it should be called to action.

They should want to find out more about your team. They should want to swim! Some teams include a coupon for a free workout in their printed material. This allows the team to track the effectiveness of a marketing material and sites of distribution.

Press Releases

Some teams maintain a regular stream of contact with newspapers and local publications through press releases. Masters swimming is newsworthy! It is considered a human interest topic. A press release can highlight a special activity of the team.

It can report on the swimming accomplishments of team members. It can cover team milestones. In addition to the main topic, each press release should also include information about joining the team and contact information. Press releases can be sent to sports editors and community events editors.

Community Participation

Some teams participate in community events, such as fairs and parades. A team that is connected to the community can be more inviting to the average person. Sometimes Masters swimming can be viewed as an exclusive group, open only to the very best and experienced swimmers. Being involved in community events is an opportunity to introduce your team with the more accurate image of Masters swimming, as an activity open to all adults looking for swimming fitness. It shows that your team is made up of regular people. It makes your team more approachable.

The Best Marketing Tool

Probably the most effective means of marketing available to a Masters swim program has no extra effort or expense associated with it. It requires no design and printing, no writing skill, and no special organization. The best form of marketing is word of mouth.

It is carried out spontaneously and with genuine enthusiasm by the members of the team. The impact of publicity through word of mouth is unparalleled. Swimmers who enjoy the experience of Masters swimming with your team, who are happy about their swimming progress, or who have made friends on the team will talk about it. This means that marketing becomes a matter of delivering on your mission statement, having smooth team operations, offering a great program with a solid schedule of swimming and excellent coaching. If you make this happen, your program will speak for itself.

FUNDRAISING

2.9

Fundraising is done for many reasons by Masters swim teams. If dues do not meet expenses, a team may fundraise for its own survival. Some teams fundraise to help keep the pool they swim at open through the winter. Some teams fundraise to help the pool purchase new equipment. Some teams fundraise and give the proceeds to a community organization. Teams organized as non-profits can offer tax-deductible receipts to donors. Team fundraisers can take many forms, including:

Swim-a-thon

A swim-a-thon is a traditional fundraiser for swim teams. Once an event date is set, swimmers get sponsors who pledge a dollar amount for every lap the swimmers will swim in the swim-a-thon event. The event is often defined as an hour swim, when spectators are invited to watch the swimmers accomplish their laps. swim-a-thons require swimmers to actively participate by gathering sponsors, collecting money, and swimming. Sometimes prizes are given for the most laps and for the most money raised. With good participation, a swim-a-thon can be a very successful fundraiser and a fun event for the team.

Silent Auction

A silent auction is popular fundraising tool for many organizations. People buy tickets for the opportunity to attend an event where items of interest are displayed. They bid in writing on items that interest them over the course of an evening dinner or party-type gathering. As the silent auction clock runs out, bidding can reach a fevered pitch! In the end, the highest bidder gets the item. This kind of event requires a great deal of advance planning, advertising, ticket sales, as well as the collection of items for the auction.

Some teams ask their members to donate items for auction. Others approach businesses in the community for donations of auction items. The quality and value of the items to be auctioned often determines the success of these kinds of events. If there is a brand new mountain bike, or set of golf clubs up for auction, it will probably attract more bidders and higher bids than second-hand items.

Eating Functions

Some teams hold pancake breakfasts, crab feeds or other family-style meal events where tickets are sold in advance. Events such as these are best held in school cafeterias or other locations with large size kitchen setups. The food and supplies can be purchased wholesale or sometimes even gathered by donation. Increased appeal can be added if a celebrity guest agrees to appear and sign autographs or make a short speech. Raffles and door prizes can also be advertised. Teams holding eating functions often have the greatest success if the event is held annually, as it becomes a fun family tradition for many ticket buyers. Eating events require a great deal of teamwork as the ticket sales, preparation, set up, cooking, serving and clean up are all done by team members.

Yard Sales

One of the easiest fundraising efforts a Masters swim team can take on is an old fashioned yard sale. Most team members have stores of treasures in their garages and attics awaiting an event like this! The combined "stuff" of your whole team makes a very appealing sale to passersby. To hold a successful yard sale, as well as donating things, team members must volunteer to transport, sort, display, price and sell the "stuff" at your yard sale. Working in shifts, no one will be overworked, and your yard sale will go well.

It is important to secure a location in a high traffic area to get the best results. Someone on your team might own a business on a main street with a visible parking lot that he or she could offer for the event. Advertising your yard sale in local newspapers can also bring in more shoppers. At the end of the day, remaining "stuff" can be donated to a local charity.

DEALING WITH CHALLENGES   2.10

Your new Masters Swim Program should be prepared to face challenges along the way. Some may be just inconvenient glitches that are easily remedied. However, some may seem insurmountable. During these times, it is important to keep in mind your motivation for starting your program and to look at all the positive aspects of being involved with your team. You must look out for the interests and future of your team. Your perseverance in hard times will make your team stronger. Some common challenges include:

Pool Politics

If you run a swim team, you will encounter pool politics. For some reason, the otherwise wonderful swim center environment also seems to be a haven for power plays and personal agendas. Establishing a good working relationship with the manager of your home pool is important, as this person makes important decisions affecting your team and program regarding pool time, budgeting, and staffing, among other issues. Keeping an open dialogue is essential. If contact is not coming to you from the pool manager, you should make contact! Being recognized as a problem solver is key. Work with your pool manager, not against him or her. Finally, since many pool managers are focused on "the bottom line," attendance figures and notes from satisfied customers are very influential. The popularity of your program can give you more clout when dealing with pool managers.

Beyond pool managers, your interactions with the various personalities around the pool are critical. Lifeguards, office staff, cashiers, even lap swimmers can make you and your team's experience at the pool either pleasant or miserable. It is important to maintain a courteous relationship with everyone around the pool. The quality and future of your program depends on you being a good pool citizen, someone who is conscientious and concerned about the larger pool community, rather than exclusively about the activities of your own program. When a problem comes up, deal with it directly, professionally and promptly. Learn the proper channels of the pool management to follow. Know who is a supporter of your program and who is not. Be ready to use your skills as a team builder to diffuse tense situations and turn them around.

Pool Problems

Problems with water temperature, chemical imbalances and no-show lifeguards can negatively affect your team. Although ensuring a working and open pool may not be your responsibility, if workouts are frequently canceled due to these kinds of problems, swimmers can become discouraged with your team and look for another team. To prevent this, you must get involved. Have the phone number of the pool maintenance person, the pool manager, and staff with you and do not hesitate to use them if a problem arises. Become a certified lifeguard yourself. If you do so, you might have more success in getting pool keys. Ask the pool staff to call you in advance if there is a pool problem so you have a chance to move the workout to another pool and advise your swimmers in advance. In cases where the pool is out of order frequently, or your team is locked out for another reasons, you might consider securing another home pool for workouts.

Poor Team Culture

A team culture where a disrespectful attitude toward the coach is allowed to manifest can be seriously damaging. When the coach is not seen as a team leader, but as someone who fetches kick boards and pulls pool covers, something is wrong. This problem can have its beginnings in the choice of coaches. The job of coaching Masters is often assigned to unengaged or inexperienced employees. With such a figure on deck, swimmers get used to the workout having no rhyme or reason. They get used to little or no technique feedback being offered. This problem can also develop when a coach's financial compensation is very low.

If a coach continually puts in countless hours of unpaid time to make the program work, his or her enthusiasm may be slowly whittled away and replaced by the feeling of being taken for granted. The consequence is less and less energy being put out by the undervalued coach. Another reason this happens is when a single athlete insists they know better than the coach on deck, and wants the coach and the rest of the team to know it too. A coach may give directions for the next set only to hear one swimmer tell another, "I am not going to do that. I have a better set." This kind of disrespect is not so uncommon. It is contagious. If the coach is seen as an unimportant, the benefits of a strong coaching presence will not occur on your team, and a good coach will not stay for long. Your team will suffer for it. A team culture that values the coach and the impact of good coaching can make the difference between a mediocre and a thriving Masters swim program.

A new coach coming onto a team with such a climate of disrespect has an uphill climb to turn things around. Some coaches will choose to walk away from a team with these kinds of dynamics, justifiably unwilling to accept the inhospitable environment.

The best approach for a coach who chooses to take on the challenge of this sort of team is to work to gain the trust and support of the swimmers one at a time. It will take patience, and lots of it. The swimmers may ignore the new coach, talk over him or her, and challenge his or her expertise. With perseverance and a strong vision, a good coach can gain the trust of the team.

2.11 MAKING IT OFFICIAL

Registering Your Team

To become an official Masters swim team, you must register your team with the Masters swimming organization in your area. Registering your team is a matter of filling out forms and paying a nominal fee. Every Masters swim team must be officially registered with their local Masters swimming committee before athletes can be registered with the team. A team must register each calendar year.

When you register your team, important information, including the team contacts, safety coordinator and coach's certifications, is compiled into the Masters swimming database. Your home pool location and workout schedule will also be recorded. Upon registering your team, you will be sent an official Masters swim team package including a certificate showing that your team is a registered Masters swim team, a rule book, and insurance information.

An overview of the organization's functions will also be included, offering opportunities for your new team to become involved in its various committees and decision making processes. Instructions on registering athletes also come in this package.

Registering Your Athletes

Once your team is registered as an official Masters swim team, it is the team's responsibility to make sure that every athlete who swims with the team is a currently registered member of Masters Swimming. This is very important because the insurance that Masters swimmers get as a benefit of membership is only valid if all swimmers are registered. It is not fair to the swimmers who register as they are supposed to do to have their insurance benefits voided because another swimmer doesn't register. Being a registered Masters swimmer is a requirement that all team members should be held to. Membership must be renewed each calendar year for a nominal fee.

Registered swimmers receive a membership card that shows the current year of registration. Registered swimmers are eligible to swim in Masters swimming competitions worldwide. They receive regular updates on Masters swimming news and events through weekly e-mails, a monthly newsletter, and bi-monthly magazine.

THE MASTERS NETWORK

2.12

Because Masters swimming is truly a worldwide phenomenon, an extensive network has developed around Masters swimming. Through both internet connections and personal interaction, this network provides swimmers with a real sense of being a part of something big. It also provides an extensive array of Masters swimming resources.

One of the most used resources is called "Places to Swim," and it is a comprehensive listing of Masters swim teams and their workout times, as well as pools offering lap swim times all over the world. Swimmers who travel for work, or who go on vacation, can make use of this resource to keep up their swimming while away from home. It is also a good resource for swimmers who are planning to relocate.

"Places to Swim" is a link that can be accessed through the United States Swimming website at www.usms.org.

The Masters swimming network online also offers the opportunity for swimmers to get information on upcoming Masters swimming competitions, conventions, rule changes, meet results, time standards, swimming records, history, current news, and other subjects of interest.

Beyond the internet, the Masters swimming network also exists through the personal connections made between Masters swimmers. Swimmers are the best resources for other swimmers in terms of referrals. Swimmers learn from each other where the best place is to buy swimming equipment, where to find an early morning workout, and what the temperature of a certain pool is.

Masters swimmers also use their network to support each other. They are known to spread the word when a fellow swimmer is ill or in crisis. They remember each other's birthdays, which are viewed as major achievements the older a Masters swimmer becomes. They actively maintain long-term friendships even if they live on separate continents.

CHAPTER 5
STICKING WITH IT

1 What Masters Swimmers Think About

Many Masters swimmers look at their swimming as "their own time," a special time when they are alone with their thoughts. But what exactly Masters swimmers think about while they swim is determined in part by the level of skill and comfort they have achieved with their swimming technique and conditioning. At first, thoughts may be cognitive in nature. The swimmer understands, in theory, what he is supposed to do, and he tries to translate that into action. Later, thoughts become more associative. Having mastered individual skills, the swimmer thinks about how to coordinate the parts. Finally, thoughts evolve to the autonomous level. When the swimmer is able to swim without thinking about it as a series of mechanical movements, thoughts can turn to other matters. Swimming becomes a time where personal matters are processed, plans are made, and thinking is done, all simultaneously with good swimming.

As an example, a person just beginning Masters swimming may think about the path of the arm stroke, or the kick, or the breathing as he or she swims a workout. Then, as this swimmer gains the skill to perform these individual aspects of the stroke, thoughts change to more complex concepts including how to coordinate the arm stroke with the breathing and kick. Then, as the swimmer's stroke comes together, while thinking about how to get more leverage out of the stroke through employing the muscles of their core, their thoughts might gravitate to reflections of the day at work or making mental notes on what is needed at the grocery store on the way home from the workout.

Likewise, with the process of conditioning, at first a swimmer thinks about how he or she is going to ever make it to the end of the pool, or how tired his or her muscles are. Then, as adaptation occurs, thoughts include matters of swimming on a regular interval or attempting longer sets. Finally, as the swimmer reaches a higher level of conditioning and accomplishing the workout is a "given," thoughts include such things as writing an overdue thank you letter to a friend or having lunch with a swimmer in the next lane.

On the surface, it may seem odd that as swimmer's technique and conditioning become better and better, swimming becomes less and less in the forefront of his or her mind. But in fact, what happens is that a swimmer's swimming becomes so integrated into his or her thoughts and actions that more than one task can be successfully accomplished at the same time. When a swimmer finds himself or herself thinking in this manner, it is an indication that a new phase of swimming has begun. It shows that all the work a swimmer has done is paying off.

2 Measuring Progress

Staying motivated is probably the single most important factor in sticking with a swimming program. Most swimmers find that in order to stay motivated, it is helpful to find ways to periodically measure their progress. Progress can be defined in many ways, and no one measure is perfect for everyone. Several options include:

2.1 GOAL SETTING

Setting personal goals is one way swimmers may stay motivated to keep swimming because goals define a path or purpose that must be accomplished over time. Goals should be realistic yet challenging. They are most useful when they do not make swimming into a pass or fail situation. In other words, avoid defining your goal by a specific date or other fixed circumstance. Let the goal be a challenge in front of you to achieve, not a source of stress.

There are short-term goals and long-term goals. Short-term goals include personal challenges that are within reach but require focus to achieve. They may be steps along the way toward a long-term goal. Long-term goals are larger challenges and require the swimmer to work on incremental but steady progress over an extended period of time. An example of short-term goals may be "I will work on improving my breaststroke kick." An example of a long-term goal could be, "I want to swim a 200 breaststroke well in competition."

Setting goals and then working to reach those goals is something that allows us to look at our swimming in terms of more than the present, but as an activity that will engage us into the future.

COMPETITION

Masters swimming offers opportunities for competition year round. Competitions are held at the local, regional, national, and international levels. Competitions are held in four seasons: short course yards, long course meters, short course meters and open water. Participating in competition is an option that is very good for measuring progress. Unfortunately, many Masters swimmers miss out on this chance to measure their progress because of the connotation that competition brings. Competition is something that we all experience in many aspects of our lives, and for many swimmers, Masters swimming is viewed as a refuge from the competition of the rest of their lives.

What Does Competition Mean to You?

Competition can be viewed in two basic ways. It can be seen as unpleasant and stressful, or as exciting and fun. It can be seen in terms of winning and losing, or it can be seen as an opportunity to do one's best. This distinction separates people who enjoy competition from people who avoid it.

When a swimmer swims against other swimmers to win, there is a real chance that it won't happen because only one person comes in first, and the other swimmers don't. Whereas, when a swimmer swims in the company of other swimmers in order to do his or her best, coming in first is not necessary to win.

A swimmer is a winner by swimming at his or her own top effort. In this second view of competition, the swim meet environment is just an opportunity when official times are taken and where swimming conditions are ideal. The pressure to come out on top and the humiliation of not being first are not part of this thinking.

Competing in Masters swimming is a unique experience that is a breath of fresh air to many swimmers. Swimmers begin their race with friendly support and unexpected encouragement from swimmers they have never even met, and they finish their races with applause and repeated congratulations from those same swimmers, who will never again be considered strangers. It is a very uplifting experience for most swimmers who try it.

For those Masters swimmers who also swam competitively as kids, going to a swim meet often yields an additional pleasant experience. An apparent stranger may approach you and call you by name. After

a perplexed moment, you may recognize him or her as a swimmer from your childhood team who, like you, has returned to the sport through Masters swimming. You may not have seen each other in 15, 20, or 25 years, but an instant kinship is present. It is wonderful to see people from your childhood still involved in swimming. You realize that swimming has truly impacted your life. You realize that swimming together so long ago was as special to your childhood teammate as it was to you, and like you, they are still at it!

What Competition Means to Your Coach

One of the biggest highlights of coaching is watching the swimmers that a coach has trained swim in a competition. If you are not motivated to measure your progress at a swim meet, you might consider going to a swim meet for this reason.

When a swimmer gets up on the block, his or her coach feels the same butterflies, the same focus, and the same flood of everything that the swimmer has done to get to this point. It is a very proud moment for a coach when a swimmer that he or she has worked with gets up on the blocks.

During the race, the coach is thrilled to watch the technique that the swimmer has developed over time in action! The coach watches as the conditioning that the swimmer has worked for at practice is tested under race conditions. The coach watches every aspect of the race, often with the hair on his or her arms standing on end!

A swimmer looking for motivation to swim in competition might want to think of the hours that his or her coach dedicates to the swimmer's improvement. Your coach stands on the deck with wet feet in the sun, in the rain, before the sun comes up, and after it goes down. Your coach is there with you. Going to a swim meet is a great way to say "thank you" to your coach.

Setting a Benchmark

The first official time that you swim at a swim meet serves as your benchmark. It gives you a starting point to build from. It will be the time you use as your entry time for your next meet. At your next swim meet, by using this time, you will be grouped with swimmers of your gender who are swimming the same event, at approximately the same speed as you, often regardless of their age.

The very first time you enter a swim meet, you must enter an estimated time, which your coach can help you with. An alternative is to use a workout time off the pace clock as your entry time.

Recording Your Times

Once you have established your first official times in competition, making a record of them is an excellent idea. Some swimmers have a diary or swim meet log in which they write down their times, the dates they swam those times, and sometimes even notes on the swim, including ways they think they could improve. Some swimmers create a spreadsheet on their computers with which they can follow their progress. Many swimmers make it a practice of swimming every event at least once a year so they can have a complete history of the progress of their swimming.

Time Standards

If a swimmer becomes involved in ongoing competition, he or she may want to be aware of certain time standards that are set by Masters swimming. Some swimmers find it motivating to have a time standard to reach for.

These time standards include qualification times to enter certain Championship meets, which are usually established by using the sixteenth fastest time for a particular event and age group from the previous year. There are "Top 10" lists for regional, national and international levels, which a swimmer can  aspire to achieve. There are Masters swimming records kept for every event and age group, and "All American" lists that can also be a source of motivation. All of these time standards can be used as a way to measure a swimmer's own progress from year to year.

Relays

Sometimes being a member of a relay team in a swim meet is a good introduction to competing in Masters swimming. Being part of a relay team takes the focus off any one swimmer, as four swimmers

swim in succession in the same race. A swimmer feels the close support of his or her teammates, and the cheerful atmosphere of a Masters swim meet, without any pressure. A swimmer who is reluctant to compete may be more inclined to do so for the team than for himself or herself.

Open Water Swimming

Open water swimming sparks the interest of many people and motivates some to keep swimming more than in the pool. Even though water is water, some swimmers see open water swimming almost as a different sport than pool swimming. In a swim meet, swimmers are separated by lanes. The water is clean and clear. There is no problem knowing which way to swim or how much distance is yet to be covered. The temperature is comfortable. Swimmers get to relax through every turn. None of this is true when swimming in a lake, the ocean or a river. For those who love the open water, this is part of the appeal.

In the open water, swimmers have to get used to being cold. Thinking about the water as refreshing, not cold, works for some swimmers! To acclimate to cold water, practice swimming in open water, steadily increasing time spent in the water. Some swimmers wear wetsuits. Others choose to experience the real thing. But in extreme conditions, even these "naturalists" wear a neoprene cap and ear plugs to insulate the head. In the open water, limited visibility makes orientation a challenge.

Choosing a landmark in advance to "sight" during a swim is a good idea. Then, by using periodic heads-up strokes swimmers will better stay on course. Race courses are usually marked by occasional red buoys but knowing how to navigate is a good skill to learn.

Swimming with plant life and even creatures is an unsettling experience at first! Thinking about swimming efficiency is a good distraction. Just ignore what could be going on beneath the surface or what is watching from down there! There is usually no chance to warm up and there are no walls to rest on. Swimmers will have to overcome waves and currents, and because they will be swimming a mile or more, establishing a sustainable pace is important.

When participating in an open water race, there will be no best times, as there are in the pool, even when a swimmer has swum the same distance in the same body of water before. The conditions and circumstances vary from race to race and from day to day so that each race is a unique experience.

The infamous mass start leaves some swimmers wondering where to best position themselves. In some races, hundreds of swimmers begin the race at the same time. No one wants to be last before the race even starts, and no one wants to be run over. Those swimmers out to win usually start at the front and center. Those who are out just have a fun time, usually start on the outside  and to the rear. Once the race begins, swimmers should expect other swimmers to crawl over them, to scratch their skin, pull their legs and push them underwater. This is the way it is in open water swimming.

Drafting is the secret weapon of many successful open water swimmers. By allowing another swimmer to take a slight lead, the swimmer drafting is drawn along with the lead swimmer. This allows the swimmer following to save his or her energy for the sprint at the finish. If you are among the faster swimmers in an open water race, expect to experience drafting. It is entirely legal. The best open water swimmers develop strategies to share the leader's role in drafting and know when it is time to break away.

Open water swimming has its own wonderful appeal. It is always an adventure, and it offers you the chance to swim in places other people only see from afar. From Alcatraz to San Francisco, across the English Channel, or to the other side of a local lake, wherever and whatever you swim, you can look back with pride and satisfaction.

CHALLENGE SETS

2.3

Swimmers may want to measure their progress in the workout environment through challenge sets. While a challenge set may take many forms, it is meant to be repeated periodically, effectively tracking a swimmer's progress over time. Because challenge sets are done as a part of a workout, they measure a swimmer's level of conditioning more directly than their speed.

One of the most popular challenge sets among swimmers and coaches is "10 x 100." In this set, the swimmer strives to make each 100 faster than they swam the previous time they did the set. Or, a swimmer may be asked to hold the same times with less rest than before.

Another common challenge set is "500 for time." In this set, a swimmer's overall swim time is measured, as well as the "splits" of each of the successive five 100s. This set is an excellent way to measure progress in overall endurance and consistency of the swimmer's pace.

Some teams get very creative with their challenge sets. A "200 Fly," or "3 x 400 I.M. at the end of workout" are challenge sets that swimmers boast about doing. Some teams schedule a regular time for challenge sets, like once a month or every Friday. Sometimes challenge sets are assigned by surprise during a workout. Challenge sets can be very motivating for the team to do together.

2.4 PHYSICAL CHANGES

Some swimmers notice positive changes in their physical appearance soon after beginning a Masters swimming routine. These changes include reduced body fat, improved muscle tone, and weight loss. These changes are not accomplished through dieting, but through ongoing physical activity of their Masters swimming routine. Dieting, in fact is not recommended, especially reduced carbohydrate diets, because swimming requires a great deal of energy output, and energy output requires readily available fuel.

Changes to a swimmer's body continue over time. As the swimmer gains more conditioning and good swimming technique, the body becomes more and more efficient at using available energy. Improvements in a swimmer's physique are the result of cumulative swimming. They are a visible measure of a swimmer's progress.

Body Fat

Swimmers can lose body fat easily with a regular Masters swimming routine. Losing fat happens when the body uses up the calories that the swimmer has in immediate fuel and accesses the body's energy storage, or fat. The body is very efficient at accessing the various energy sources it has available, but it does so in a particular order. Some swimmers might wonder, "why not speed up the process by just not consuming calories, so the fat storage is accessed immediately?" This idea just does not work. Doing so deprives the body of the primary energy source it pulls from, especially for exercise. If calories are not readily available when a swimmer works out, the body signals itself to go into "starvation mode." This is a survival measure of the body that slows down the metabolism of a person exercising without calories, so that only a bare minimum of fat storage is used. The body, thinking that it is being starved, attempts to preserve more fat for later, ensuring that the body can survive for a longer time.

A swimmer working out in starvation mode will go into a workout feeling depleted and not have the energy necessary to perform a workout well enough to make the conditioning process occur. In addition, fat loss is actually slowed down. For swimmers, consuming an average 2000 calorie per day diet, fat loss usually happens without extra measures. It happens while the swimmer is enjoying his or her swimming.

Fat loss also happens for swimmers in another way. The constant pressure of the water on the swimmer's body produces a mild compression effect. Swimmers notice reduced cellulite with regular immersion and activity.

All this being said, studies measuring body composition, or percentage of body fat show that among fit athletes, swimmers are not generally the leanest athletes. Runners and gymnasts are generally measured with less body fat than swimmers. However, the standard methods of measuring body fat do not distinguish between "white fat" and "brown fat." While the lean muscle mass of swimmers is largely the same as those athletes measured with the least percentage of body fat, swimmers have "brown fat."

"Brown fat" is a thin, insulating layer commonly seen in people living in very cold climates. It is also seen in the cheeks of infants. In swimmers, the purpose of "brown fat" is generally attributed to extended periods of immersion in water of a temperature colder than the average human body temperature. "Brown fat" has a very beneficial effect for swimmers, beyond insulation. It provides improved floatation, allowing forward motion with less effort and less drag.

Muscle Tone

Because swimming uses nearly every muscle group in the body, improvement in muscle tone is noticeable quite quickly. Swimmers may see more definition in their arms, abdomens and legs. This is a welcome sight to most adult swimmers!

An added benefit of improving muscle tone is that muscle fiber carries blood more efficiently than fat, so cardiovascular improvement happens at a faster rate when muscles are toned. The consequence is that a swimmer with toned muscles feels more energetic both in and out of the pool.

Weight Loss

Initially, swimmers may be alarmed to find that their weight actually increases when they first become involved in a Masters swimming routine. This happens because muscle weighs more than fat. But as muscles become stronger, the capacity of the body to do more work increases, and so more energy is used, causing eventual loss of fat, and therefore loss of weight.

Weight loss occurs when the body has weight to lose. Swimmers will usually balance out at a healthy athletic weight. Measuring one's progress in swimming should not be a matter of how thin a swimmer can become, but instead, how healthy and fit he or she can become.

3 Making a Routine that Works

Swimming is most rewarding in terms of technique improvements, progress in conditioning, and enjoyment when it is done regularly. It is therefore important for every swimmer to find a routine that works for him or her. Working out an average of three or four times per week is a good amount of swimming. Creating a working schedule that includes three to four workouts per week is a very individual thing. Finding what works might require some trial and error, but once swimming becomes a real routine, a swimmer will find that it was well worth it.

A.M. AND P.M. SWIMMERS

3.1

Many swimmers report that they swim better in the morning than the evening, or better at the end of the day than at the start. Certain swimmers feel more energetic at specific times in their day. Getting to know the high and low points of one's own energy flow can help establish a routine that makes swimming more rewarding. Trying both early and late workouts might reveal a definite difference in the degree of motivation that a swimmer has to come to a workout and the level of energy he or she has to do that workout. Finding the best time of day for one's own body to do exercise can be an important factor in sticking with a swimming routine.

LOOKING PAST EXCUSES

3.2

During the process of establishing a workout routine, there might be times when a swimmer is unmotivated to stick to the schedule. At these times, it is easy to convince oneself that there is a good reason for not going swimming. Maybe it is "I had to stay up too late last night," or "I have to run an errand." When a swimmer finds himself or herself coming up with a reason not to swim, it is important to remember that it might in fact just be an excuse. Try to recognize what is happening and take a moment to think about it. Look past today, when you might be feeling a bit tired or sore. Look toward the day when you are a confident, fit, efficient swimmer.

Keep in the front of your mind that each day you swim is a stepping stone in that direction. Look at your swimming as your own special time, that it is a priority and a rewarding experience to you in so many ways. Look past the excuses and give yourself the gift of swimming. Remember, you always feel better after a workout.

3.3 SOLVING PROBLEMS

Sometimes there are real issues that stand between you and your swimming. Maybe you have no childcare for your baby. Maybe you have a deadline at work. This is part of life. How you deal with problems that arise is also a part of life. All swimmers encounter issues that get in the way of their swimming routine. The way to deal with them is to become a problem solver. You can't ignore the responsibilities in your life in order to swim. You have to find a way to make it all work. Do what it takes! Become adaptable. Do what you have to do and swim at an alternate time, or even the next day. Combine resources with other swimmers, such as babysitting or carpooling. Don't give up! It is a major achievement to make it all work.

3.4 GIVE IT THREE WEEKS

Adjusting to the demands of a new workout routine, developing a routine that works for you, and making your swimming a real part of your life takes time. It might be tempting during the initial stage to go back to your old way of life, which probably seems less complicated and easier. But there comes a time, somewhere around three weeks after you have started your new fitness routine, when something seems to click.

You notice that swimming becomes significantly easier. You notice that going to each workout becomes something you look forward to. You notice that you have developed the ability to get everything done. You notice that you have made new friends. The challenge is to make it through those first three weeks. For some new swimmers, it may help to look at the swimmers beside you, stroking easily through the water, happy with the balance of health, family and career that they have achieved. They have reached the point where swimming actually improves the other aspects of their lives. And without their swimming, they would feel as if something was missing in their life. You, too, can get to that point. It is a matter of just three weeks. When you reach this point, the world of Masters swimming will be a part of you.

LAST WORD

Now that you have reached the end of this Masters simming manual, it is our hope that you have found new information and inspiration to get in the swim. We hope that you open the book again, from time to time, using it to build your swimming and fitness. Above all, we hope you use it to find your place in Masters swimming.

Here is to your health! Ready ... go!

Blythe and Cornelia

REFERENCES

■ American Red Cross, *Fundamentals of Instructor Training*, 2000

■ Bleul, Cornelia, *Landtraining von Schwimmern im langfristigen Leistungsaufbau*. Unpublished scientific dissertation, Berlin, 1990

■ Bleul-Gohlke, Cornelia, *Wassergymnastik*. 2nd edition. Limpert 2000

■ Clayton, Charles, M.D., editor, *American Medical Association Home Medical Encyclopedia*, Random House, New York, 1989

■ Colwin, Cecil, M., *Breakthrough Swimming*, Human Kinetics, Illinois, 2002

■ Counsilman, J. E., *The Science of Swimming*, Prentice Hall, New Jersey, 1968

■ Knebel, K. P., *Funktionsgymnastik*. Reinbek bei Hamburg, 1988

■ Maglischo, Ernest, W., *Swimming Even Faster*, Mayfield Publishing, California, 1993

■ Quick, Richard, *Championship Video Series*, Championship Productions, Iowa, 2004

■ Reischle, Klaus, *Besser Schwimmen – Technik, Training*. Oberhachingen 1988

■ usms.org, Web site of United States Swimming

■ Whitten, Phillip, *The Complete Book of Swimming*, Random House, New York, 1994

Photo & Illustration Credits

- Cover Photo: Imago Sportfotodienst GmbH, Germany
- Cover Design: Jens Vogelsang, Germany
- Photos: by Cornelia Bleul-Gohlke
- Background images: gettyimages Digital Vision
- Drawings in Chapter 1 by Cornelia Bleul-Gohlke
- Drawings in Chapter 3 by Blythe Lucero